Praise for Sri Chinmoy

"I am so pleased with all the good work you are doing for world peace and for people in so many countries. May we continue to work together and to share together all for the Glory of God and for the good of man."

—Mother Teresa,
   Nobel Peace Laureate

"Your loving heart and profound wisdom are a matter of my boundless admiration."

—Mikhail Gorbachev,
   former President of the USSR and Nobel Peace Laureate

"What you are doing is in the interest of the entire humanity and the world."

—Nelson Mandela,
   President of South Africa and Nobel Peace Laureate

"I would like to hail once again your invaluable contributions to world peace and human togetherness, which are a source of pride and inspiration for political action worldwide. Please accept my sincere thanks for what you are doing for the betterment of mankind."

—Javier Pérez de Cuéllar,
   former Secretary-General of the United Nations

"Sri Chinmoy has been a dedicated servant of peace who has been able to bring diverse people together for noble goals. At a time when war continues to rage, violence exists between races, and governments still violate basic human rights, Sri Chinmoy's message of peace is timely and inspirational."

—Paul Simon,
   United States Senator, Illinois

"Sri Chinmoy is a miraculous model of the abundance in the creative life, and I can only hope that I may someday participate in that cosmic fountain of stillness and profound energy which he inhabits."

—the late Leonard Bernstein,
   composer and conductor

"He has no ego; it is all honest feeling. Sri Chinmoy's music is a magical flow deep down in your heart of hearts."

—Addwitiya Roberta Flack,
   six-time Grammy Award winner

"By reminding people throughout the world of the importance of striving for peace on a daily basis, the Sri Chinmoy Peace-Blossoms serve a most valuable purpose."

—the late Linus Pauling,
   Nobel Peace Laureate and Nobel Laureate in Chemistry

"The word 'peace' is not simply a grouping of letters, but a living entity which must be nurtured if it is to flourish. . . . With every blossom that Sri Chinmoy helps to foster, the dream of world peace becomes a more viable reality."

—John Kerry,
   United States Senator, Massachusetts

"Sri Chinmoy, you're an inspiration to all of us."

—Carl Lewis,
  eight-time Olympic Gold Medalist

"Your accomplishments show us that the only limitations to the body and the spirit are the limitations which we place upon ourselves. May the love that you hold for mankind extend from the soul through the body into a real and lasting peace."

—Brian Mulroney,
  former Prime Minister of Canada

"I believe very much in what you do. I am an admirer of yours. I love what you're doing."

—the late Jesse Owens,
  four-time Olympic Gold Medalist

"Sri Chinmoy is a man of peace, a man of faith, and a man of God. He has done so much in the past twenty-five years to make a better world for all of us. The world badly needs more peaceful and loving men like Sri Chinmoy. Sri Chinmoy is doing so much for the world, for people of all faiths, because of his own peace and faith."

—Muhammad Ali,
  three-time World Heavyweight Boxing Champion

"Thank you very much for all your work."

—Archbishop Desmond Tutu,
  Head, Anglican Church in South Africa

A Fireside Book

PUBLISHED BY SIMON & SCHUSTER

FINDING YOUR PATH TO INNER PEACE

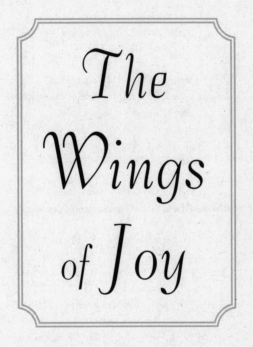

The Wings of Joy

Sri Chinmoy

FIRESIDE
Rockefeller Center
1230 Avenue of the Americas
New York, NY 10020

FIRESIDE and colophon are registered
trademarks of Simon & Schuster Inc.

Designed by Jennifer Ann Daddio
Manufactured in the United States of America

15 17 19 20 18 16 14

Library of Congress Cataloging-in-Publication Data
Chinmoy, Sri, 1931
The wings of joy: finding your path to inner peace / Sri Chinmoy.
p.   cm.
1. Spiritual life.   2. Meditation.   3. Joy—Religious aspects.
4. Peace of mind—Religious aspects.   I. Title.
BL624.C4752   1997
294.5'44—dc20   96-32387
ISBN 0-684-82242-3

Contents

Contents

Preface

My dear friends, my brothers and sisters, I am a man of prayer; I am a student of peace. I am praying to the Heavenly Father to bring to the fore all your divine qualities and to increase them in boundless measure. I am praying to God to bestow upon each of you His Dream-Message, which is peace. And I am also praying to Him to give you joy in infinite measure.

I feel it is through prayer, meditation, and dedicated service that world peace can take place. Each individual has to try to make others happy, for it is only through happiness that we can have peace. If we can offer happiness to someone lovingly and sincerely, then that person will have only goodwill toward us. So from happiness we get peace, and from peace we get happiness. The two are inseparable.

Unfortunately, this world of ours has not yet seen the face or felt the heart of peace. Why? Precisely because we are trying to bring about peace only with our mind's brilliance and splendor. As long as we try to establish peace on the strength of our mind's capacities, we shall sadly fail. We shall succeed only when we exercise our heart's capacities.

The experiences of the heart strengthen us, expand our horizons, and make us feel that we are all one family with only one home. Each individual is a pilgrim. With our wings of joy and our ever-new dreams, let us fly in the sky of love and promise. With our love we shall see and feel the world as our very own. With our promise we shall increase the beauty and divinity of all human beings and all nations.

With utmost humility, sincerity, and soulfulness, I pray to our Heavenly Father to bless us with a new millennium of dreams that will elevate the consciousness of humanity and make each and every human being supremely perfect.

CHAPTER ONE

Living in Joy

True inner joy is self-created.
It does not depend on outer circumstances.
A river is flowing in and through you carrying the message of joy.
This divine joy is the sole purpose of life.

We are all seekers, and our goal is the same: to achieve inner peace, light, and joy, to become inseparably one with our Source, and to lead lives full of true satisfaction.

To live in joy is to live the inner life. This is the life that leads to self-realization. Self-realization is God-realization, for God is nothing other than the Divinity that is deep inside each one of us, waiting to be discovered and revealed. We may also refer to God as the Inner Pilot or the Supreme. But no matter which term we use, we mean the Highest within us, that which is the ultimate goal of our spiritual quest.

Only if we feed the inner life can the outer life have real meaning. Three times a day we feed the body without fail. But again, there is deep inside us a divine child called our soul; we do not find time to feed this child. The soul is the conscious representative of God in us. Unless and until the soul-child is fulfilled, we can never be fulfilled in our outer life.

How do we make the connecting link between the inner life and the outer life? If we know the divine art of meditation, easily and consciously we can unite these two worlds. When we practice meditation, each moment becomes a golden opportunity to cast aside depression, frustration, anger, fear, and other negative qualities and to bring forward the divine qualities of the inner world: love, peace, joy, and light.

A spiritual person should be a normal person, a sound person. In order to reach God, a spiritual person has to be divinely practical in his day-to-day activities. In divine practicality, we share our inner wealth. We feel the divine motivation behind each action and share the result with others. Spirituality does not negate the outer life. The outer life should be the manifestation of the divine life within us.

Consciousness: The Spark of Life

Consciousness is the spark of life that unites each one of us with the Universal Life. It is the link between God and man, between Heaven and earth. Without consciousness, everything is a barren desert. When we enter into a dark place, we take a flashlight to see where we are going. If we want to know about our unlit life, we have to take the help of consciousness.

Consciousness is like a ladder. You can go up and down the various rungs. If you can meditate deeply, each plane of consciousness will present itself before you. The first rung is the physical body. The second rung is the vital. The vital is a term used in Indian philosophy. It embodies emotional, aggressive, and dynamic qualities. The third rung is the mind. Above the mind is the spiritual heart. It is in the spiritual heart that one feels the "quickening" of the soul. The soul is the self-effulgent messenger of God within us. It knows no birth, no decay, no death. It is eternal. It is immortal. It came directly from God, it remains in contact with God, and it will go back to God.

Before taking human incarnation, the soul gets an inner message about its divine purpose on earth. It is fully conscious of its mission. But during our lifetime, the workings of the physical mind may sometimes cover up the divine inspiration of the soul and its true purpose. Then the mission of the soul cannot come forward. Only if we aspire with the mind, heart, and soul can we learn the purpose of our existence here on earth.

My soul is in charge of my glowing deeds.
My heart is in charge of my soaring feelings.
My mind is in charge of my transforming thoughts.
My vital is in charge of my flowing energy.
My body is in charge of my striving life.

The Inner Cry

Aspiration is the mounting cry, the climbing cry inside our heart. We can enter into the divine consciousness through our inner cry. This cry is not for name and fame. This cry is for our total, unconditional, unreserved oneness with God, who is the Inner Pilot of our life-boat.

Some people are totally oblivious to the Inner Pilot. Again, some know of the existence of the Inner Pilot, but they do not want to have any connection or communion with Him. A sincere seeker feels the necessity of constant communion with the Inner Pilot. He is not satisfied by just knowing of God's existence inside him. He wants to be in God's consciousness and commune with Him twenty-four hours a day.

We have to make God a living reality in our day-to-day lives. We have to feel that God's presence is of paramount importance. If we do not eat every day, we starve our body. Similarly, we have to feel that if we do not pray and meditate every day, then we are starving our spiritual body. When we aspire with our heart's tears, we see that God is coming down to us, descending from above. It is just like two persons meeting; one is on the first floor and the other is on the third floor. We go up to the second floor, and God comes down to the second floor. There we meet and fulfill each other.

The stairway to the second floor is created by our heart's cry. This is the cry of aspiration; it is not like shedding tears when you do the wrong thing. The heart is crying and yearning like a mounting flame burning upward, always rising. God descends with His Grace, like a river running downward. When aspiration and Grace meet together, we come to experience the divine fulfillment of union with God.

No, it is not possible
For any inner cry
To remain unheard.

Becoming a Spiritual Potter

If we accept the spiritual life in the true sense of the term, we do not renounce the world or try to escape from the world. We embrace the world and try to fulfill the world in a divine way, in the way that God wants. I do not see eye-to-eye with those who say that God is only in Heaven and not elsewhere. God is in Heaven, and God is also on earth. The Creator can never be separated from His creation. This world of ours is His creation. He is here. He abides within all things.

We have to accept the world as it is. If we do not accept something, how are we going to transform it? If the potter does not touch the lump of clay, how is he going to shape it into a pot? If his aim is to make a pot or pitcher, he has to touch the clay. This clay is the world. We have to transform the face of the world on the strength of our dedication to the divinity in humanity.

Do not think that by praying to God or meditating on God, you are caring only for yourself and not for the rest of humanity. If you go to the foot of the creation-tree, you will see that God is the root. If you water the root of the tree, then the creation-tree will grow the way the divine Law wants it to. The concern you show for the root of the tree, for God, will feed all the branches, which will then live according to God's Perfection.

God-realization means self-discovery in the highest sense of the term. One consciously realizes his oneness with God. As long as a seeker remains unrealized, he will feel that God is somebody else who has infinite Power, while he, the seeker, is the feeblest person on earth. But the moment he realizes God, he comes to know that he and God are absolutely one in both the inner and the outer life. God-realization means one's identification with one's absolute highest Self.

Each individual has to realize God according to his inner capacity. And each individual can choose to accept the aspect of God that pleases him most. Somebody may like God's personal aspect—God as a most luminous Being—while another person may like the impersonal aspect—God as infinite Energy. Again, somebody else will be pleased only if the God he realizes is a God beyond his imagination. God is both personal and impersonal. God will come to each individual according to that individual's choice, to please him in his own way.

God is both masculine and feminine. The term "Father" is more commonly used for God in the Western world. In the East, we quite often speak of the Supreme Goddess. But when I am with Westerners, I use the term which is more familiar to you, because I feel that it will be easier for me to share my experiences with you in that way.

One can practice spirituality irrespective of which religion one belongs to. Religion may be compared to a house. You may live in one house, and I may live in another house. Although we live in different houses, we both want to learn the same subject, which is God-realization. So we both go to the same school, an inner school. When we pray to God and meditate on God, we go to this inner school. In order to go to the school, we may or may not walk along the same road. But both of us do leave our respective houses when we go to study.

A true spiritual seeker will have the deepest respect and utmost reverence for all religions. We can treasure *all* religions and claim them as our very own. Each religion is like a branch of the God-tree. How can we deny the value of the branches when we accept the tree as our very own? *Each* religion is right, absolutely right, in its own way, but when we cry for the highest Truth, love of God becomes our only religion.

True spirituality will not demand the renunciation of any religion. If you remain in your own religion and practice the spiritual life, you will be able to run very fast toward the goal. Your own religion will give you constant confidence in what you are doing. Again, you may feel the need to transcend religion. In either case, your goal is to realize God, who embodies all religions and, at the same time, is far above them.

Self-awakening
Means
God-flowering
In and through me.

Start Here and Now

In order to become one with God, you have to consciously start your spiritual journey. Here and Now is the soul's motto. If you have not yet started, then your soul wants you to start your spiritual journey at this very moment. If you have doubt with regard to God's existence, no harm. Doubt as much as you want to. Eventually, you will become tired of doubting God. If you doubt the existence of inner peace and bliss, doubt as long as you want to. Even if you have doubts with regard to the inner life or God's reality, it is best to start your inner journey anyway.

If you are curious to know what spirituality is, you can accept spirituality with your utmost curiosity. See if it is just superficially fascinating or if it is something deep and vast, to which you can devote your entire life. You may start with curiosity, but soon your curiosity will turn into real aspiration. If you enter the spiritual life because others have done so, this is also fine. If you see that somebody's life has become peaceful and happy after he has accepted the spiritual life, there is nothing wrong with imitating him.

I wish to tell you a favorite story of the great spiritual Master Sri Ramakrishna. Once a thief entered into a palace at midnight and overheard a conversation between the king and the queen. The king said to the queen, "I wish our youngest daughter to marry a holy man so that she will have some peace. All our other daughters have married kings and generals, but their lives are miserable. The holy men have a very peaceful life, so if she marries one of them, her life will be full of peace. Tomorrow, early in the morning, I shall send my ministers to the banks of the Ganges, where many holy men meditate. I am sure that one of them will agree to marry our daughter."

The thief overheard the conversation and thought: "My God, a poor monk will get the princess? Let me go there and meditate with the monks. Who knows, perhaps I may be selected. Now I have to steal in order to get a little money. But if the princess is satisfied with me, then I will become rich overnight. I will be flooded with material prosperity."

Early the next morning, dressed in the garb of a holy man, the thief went to the Ganges and started meditating with the other monks. Soon the king's ministers arrived and began going from one monk to the next seeking one who would marry the princess. The monks became furious. "We are crying for infinite light, infinite truth, infinite joy, and you want to bind us to this world again? We do not want the material life or material possessions!" they shouted. The poor ministers got rebukes and scoldings from all the monks. The monks cared not for the princess; they cared only for the highest Truth and inner wealth.

One by one, the monks gave their refusals. Finally, when the ministers came to the thief, he agreed to accept the king's daughter. They went back to the king and narrated the whole story. On hearing that one monk had shown some interest in the princess, the king was overjoyed. "Tomorrow I shall bring my daughter to the banks of the Ganges where the holy men are praying and meditating," he said.

During the night, a divine thought entered into the mind of the thief. He thought to himself: "I am only pretending to be a holy man. Just by pretending, I am getting the princess and so much wealth and material prosperity. If I really and sincerely become a monk, I am sure that I will get infinite power, infinite light, infinite bliss, infinite peace, as these genuine monks will also eventually get from God. Why should I be attached to this finite material wealth when I have the opportunity to get infinite light, bliss, and power from God's infinite wealth?"

So the thief changed his mind during the night, and when the king approached him the following morning, he showed no respect for the king. He flared up and said, "O King, do not bind me to this material world. I want God and God alone. I do not need your daughter." The poor king went back to his palace, and the thief became a sincere holy man.

This story makes it clear that at any moment we can start our spiritual journey. The thief began with imitation. But he received inspiration when he saw the real holy men crying sincerely for God and God alone. From inspiration he entered into aspiration. He was no longer satisfied with his desire to have money and material wealth, because he felt that there was something even more fulfilling to be gained.

If you still cherish doubt or curiosity, then start with doubt, start with curiosity. But start! Step-by-step, you will be able to march toward your goal. God is already eager to have you. You may not be eager to have God, but God the eternal Father, God the eternal Mother, is crying for you. You must make the decision that you want God. If you really want God, then start where you are—here and now. The goal of conscious oneness with God the infinite Light and infinite Truth shall be yours.

> *Your heart's cry is a real treasure.*
> *Your heart's cry flies like an eagle*
> *To reach the highest goal of your purest soul.*

CHAPTER TWO

Meditation: The Key to the Inner Life

Sometimes I must be silent,
For that is the only way
To know a little better,
To think a little wiser,
To become a little more perfect,
To claim God a little sooner.

Meditation is a divine gift. Meditation simplifies our outer life and energizes our inner life. Meditation gives us a natural and spontaneous life, a life that becomes so natural and spontaneous that we cannot breathe without being conscious of our own divinity.

The difference between prayer and meditation is this: when we pray, we feel that our existence is a one-pointed flame soaring upward. The very nature of prayer is to reach God by going up. When we meditate, we throw ourselves into a vast expanse, into an infinite sea of peace and bliss, or we welcome the infinite Vast into us.

Prayer and meditation are like the obverse and reverse of the same coin. Both are most effective. When I pray, I talk and God listens. When I meditate, God talks and I listen. When we pray, we go up to God; when we meditate, God comes down to us. Ultimately, they are the same. We have to know, however, that when we pray, we feel that we as individuals are separated from God. We feel that He is somewhere and that we are somewhere else. We are looking up at Him and crying to Him, but we do not know when or to what extent God is going to fulfill our prayers. Meditation says, "God is not blind or deaf! He knows what He has to do to fulfill Himself in and through me. Let me remain in soulful silence." The highest prayer was uttered by the Savior Christ: "Let Thy Will be done." This prayer is also the beginning of meditation. Where prayer stops its journey, meditation begins.

Meditation is like going to the bottom of the sea, where everything is calm and tranquil. On the surface of the sea there may be a multitude of waves, but the sea is not affected below. In its deepest depths, the sea is all silence. When we start meditating, first we try to reach our own inner existence, our true existence—that is to say, the bottom of the sea. Then, when the waves come from the outside world, we are not affected. Fear, doubt, worry, and all the earthly turmoils just wash away, because inside us is solid peace. Thoughts cannot touch us, because our mind is all peace, all silence, all oneness. Like fish in the sea, they jump and swim but leave no mark. When we are in our highest meditation, we feel that we are the sea, and the animals in the sea cannot affect us. We feel that we are the sky, and all the birds flying past cannot affect us. Our mind is the sky and our heart is the infinite sea. This is meditation.

I pray to God and meditate on God.
I pray to God to see His Face of Height.
I meditate on God to feel His Heart of Delight.

The Wings of Joy

Beginning Meditation

When you meditate at home, set aside a corner of your room which you can make absolutely pure and sanctified—a sacred place that you use only for meditation. For your daily meditation, it is best to meditate alone. Before beginning your meditation, it is helpful to take a shower or proper bath. It is also advisable to wear clean and light clothes.

To follow the spiritual life, you should meditate at least once a day. It is best to meditate early in the morning when the atmosphere is calm and peaceful. Evening is another good time. If you give importance to your meditation and are sincere, your power of meditation will automatically increase. If you are regular and punctual in your meditation, you will notice your own progress. Having a set time to meditate will help you fight against the lethargy and waywardness of the mind.

When meditating, it is important to keep the spine straight and erect, and to keep the body relaxed. You will find that your inner being will spontaneously take you to a comfortable position; it is up to you to maintain it. Some seekers like to meditate while lying down, but this is not advisable. You may easily enter into the world of sleep or into a kind of inner doze. Again, the lotus position, which is an advanced yoga posture, is not necessary for proper meditation. Many people meditate very well while they are seated in a chair.

It will help if you burn incense and candles and keep some flowers in front of you. The outer flower will remind you of the flower inside your heart. When you smell the scent of incense, you will gain inspiration and purification to add to your inner treasure. When you see the outer flame, immediately you will feel your inner flame climbing high, higher, highest.

Proper Breathing

Proper breathing is very important in meditation. When breathing, try to inhale as slowly and quietly as possible, so that if somebody placed a tiny thread in front of your nose, it would not move at all. And try to exhale more slowly still. If possible, leave a short pause between the end of your exhalation and the beginning of your inhalation. If you can, hold your breath for a few seconds. But if it is difficult, do not do it. Never do anything that will harm your organs or respiratory system.

Each time you breathe in, try to feel that you are bringing into your body infinite peace. When you breathe out, try to feel that you are expelling the restlessness within and all around you. After practicing this a few times, try to feel that you are inhaling power from the universe. When you exhale, feel that all your fear is leaving your body. After doing this a few times, try to feel that what you are breathing in is infinite joy, and what you are breathing out is sorrow, suffering, and depression.

There is also something else that you can try. Feel that you are breathing in not air, but cosmic energy. Feel that there is not a single place in your body that is not being filled by cosmic energy. It is flowing like a river inside you, washing and purifying your whole being. Then, when you start to breathe out, feel that you are breathing out all the rubbish inside you—all your undivine thoughts, obscure ideas, and impure actions.

Invite Your Friends

If you prefer a particular aspect of God—love, for instance—inwardly repeat the word "love" most soulfully several times. While uttering the word "love," try to feel that it is reverberating in the inmost recesses of your heart: "love, love, love." If you care more for divine peace, inwardly chant or repeat the word "peace." While doing this, try to hear the cosmic sound that the word embodies. Feel that "peace" is a seed-sound reverberating in the very depths of your heart. If you want light, then repeat "light, light, light" most soulfully and feel that you have actually become light. From the soles of your feet to the crown of your head, try to feel that you have become the word that you are repeating. Feel that your entire body is flooded with love, peace, and light.

One more exercise: feel that you are standing at your heart's door and that you have invited love, peace, light, delight, and all your other divine friends to enter. If complexity, insincerity, impurity, insecurity, doubt, and other negative forces appear, do not let them enter. Try to feel that both the divine qualities and the undivine qualities have taken the form of human beings, and that you can see them with your human eyes. If every day you can think of even one friend and invite that friend to enter through your heart's door, it will be the beginning of a divine friendship. One day you will allow only your friend love to come in; the next day you will allow your friend joy to come in. After some time, you will have the capacity to invite in more than one friend at a time. In the beginning, you may not have enough means to feed more than one friend at a time, but eventually you will be able to invite in all your divine friends.

Meditating on the Heart

It is better to meditate on the heart than to meditate in the mind. The mind is like Times Square on New Year's Eve; the heart is like a remote cave in the Himalayas. If you meditate in the mind, you will be able to meditate for perhaps five minutes; and out of that five minutes, for one minute you may meditate powerfully. First you may get joy and satisfaction, but then you may feel a barren desert, or your mind will be crowded with thoughts once more. But if you meditate on the heart, you acquire the capacity to identify yourself with the joy and satisfaction that you get, and then it becomes permanently yours.

There is a vast difference between what you can get from the mind and what you can get from the heart. The mind by nature is limited; the heart is unlimited. Deep within you are infinite peace, light, and bliss. To get a limited quantity is an easy task. Meditation in the mind can give it to you. But you can get infinitely more if you meditate on the heart. Suppose you have the opportunity to work at two places. At one place you will earn two hundred dollars and at the other place five hundred dollars. If you are wise, you will not waste your time at the first place.

When you meditate, feel that you are a child standing in a flower garden. This flower garden is your heart. A child can play in a garden for hours. He will go from this flower to that flower, but he will not leave the garden because he will get joy from the beauty and fragrance of each flower. Feel that inside you is a garden and you can stay in it for as long as you want. In this way you can meditate on the heart.

Your mind has a flood of questions.
There is but one teacher
Who can answer them.
Who is that teacher?
Your silence-loving heart.

Am I Meditating Correctly?

If you are meditating properly, you will feel spontaneous inner joy and peace within and without. But if you feel mental tension or disturbance, then the kind of meditation that you are doing is not meant for you. If you have a good meditation, you will have a good feeling for the world. You will see the world in a loving way in spite of its teeming imperfections. Also, if you have a dynamic feeling right after your meditation, if you feel that you have come into the world to do something and become something—to grow into God's very image and become His dedicated instrument—this indicates that you have had a good meditation.

Please do not be disturbed if you cannot meditate well in the beginning. Even in the outer life, God alone knows how many years one must practice in order to become very good at something. If an accomplished pianist thinks of what his standard was when he first began to play, he will laugh. It is through gradual progress that he has achieved his present musical height. In the spiritual life also, you may find it difficult to meditate in the beginning, but gradually your capacity will increase.

Again, right from the very first day, you will feel the benefits of meditation. When we drink even a drop of water from the earthly sea, it tastes salty. In the same way, during our meditation, if we can drink even a tiny drop from the sea of peace, we shall definitely experience peace in our lives.

Is Meditation Practical?

We say somebody is practical when he does the right thing at the right moment, so that his outer life runs smoothly. But no matter how clever we are, how conscious we are, at times we are at a loss in the outer life. We do not know what to say or do. Or, despite our saying and doing the right thing, everything goes wrong. We cannot manage our lives. We sincerely want to do something or become something, but we cannot do it.

Why does this happen? It happens because our outer capacity is always bound by our inner awareness. If we are practical in the inner life, that is to say, if we pray and meditate, then we will increase our inner awareness. When we have inner awareness, we have free access to infinite truth and everlasting joy, and we are able to control our outer life.

We always grow from within, not from without. It is from the seed under the ground that a plant grows, not vice versa. The inner life constantly carries the message of Truth and God. This inner Truth is the seed. When we allow the seed to germinate, to grow into a plant, and finally to become a tree, we can eat the fruit that the tree bears. While we are eating it, we will know that this fruit belongs to the outer world, although its source is the inner world. We will see the capacity of the inner world being manifested in the outer world.

No matter how many hours we work, or talk, or do anything in the outer world, we will not approach the Truth. But if we meditate first, and afterward act and speak, then we are doing the practical thing. The inner practicality must guide the outer life, not the other way around. The life-breath of the outer life has to come from the inner life. Only then can we be truly practical.

If we are brave enough to enter into the inner life, we will see that the inner world is practical, real, and natural. Love, light, peace, and joy are divinely normal. If we bring forward what the inner world can offer, then the outer world will also become divinely normal, practical, and fulfilling.

The Highest Reality

For a beginner, meditation seems to be the highest reality, but when one becomes an advanced seeker, one knows that meditation only leads to the highest reality. The highest reality is something one achieves or grows into while walking along the path of meditation. The divine life is not beyond our reach here on earth. The fulfillment of Divinity here on earth can never remain beyond our reach if we know the secret of secrets. That secret is to grow into divine love, where the lover and the Beloved become one, the creation and the Creator become one, the finite and the Infinite become one. When illumination dawns in a human being, God is no longer just a promise, but an actual achievement.

You can change your life. You need not wait years or even months for this change. It begins the moment you dive into the sea of spirituality. Try to live the life of spiritual discipline for a day, a single day. You are bound to succeed.

I shall now call myself;
I shall now call.
In the forest of my heart, seeing myself,
I shall love myself and love myself.
I shall be my own quest,
My absolute wealth.
The journey of light supreme will commence
In the heart of freedom.

CHAPTER THREE

Doubt-Poison and Faith-Nectar

Deepen your faith in yourself.
Nothing will be able
To frighten or weaken you.

Like every good quality, faith is a gift from God. But faith can also be increased by our personal effort. If we pray or meditate, we can increase our faith. Faith is like a muscle. If we take exercise, we develop our muscles. Similarly, if we exercise our faith, this can also be expanded. Many enter into the spiritual life out of curiosity. They have very little faith. Yet something compels them to continue.

Later on they feel within themselves the blossoming of deeper faith. When one follows a spiritual path, one is bound to acquire more faith.

One way to develop more faith is by mixing with someone who already has faith. It is like mixing with a person who has more knowledge than you have; it brings to the fore your own knowledge. Similarly, while mixing with one who has more faith, your faith-flame will be kindled. If you feel that somebody has more faith in God than you have, then go ahead and mix with that person. Even if you do not get the opportunity to talk to him, his very presence will increase the faith within you. It is advisable for you as a seeker to mix with those who have more capacity and more aspiration than you. Your heart will unconsciously act like a divine magnet to draw from them their divine qualities.

Inner Enemies and Friends

Doubt is the worst possible thief in our inner life. It takes away all our precious inner wealth. Doubt is a slow poison. Why? Because doubt starts doubting itself. Today you doubt someone and tomorrow you doubt yourself. Today you come to one conclusion and tomorrow another wave of doubt envelops you. That does not mean that today's doubt has been washed away. No, it has only been replaced by another doubt.

You have kept doubt as your friend for a very long time. If you did not feel that doubt is your real friend, you would not have stayed with doubt. But the moment you see that a better friend is entering into your life, you will not act like a fool. You will say, "Now another friend has come into my life, and I see that this friend will take me to a higher goal."

Your new friends are faith and courage. These two friends have always been beside you, but you have not sided with them. If you do change friends, what happens? In the beginning, your old friends, fear and doubt, will try to bring you back. They will not want to lose your friendship. But soon they will feel that it is beneath their dignity to mix with you. They will say, "All right, let him go, let him go. If he does not care for us, if he does not need us, then we also do not need him." It is like human pride. When we lose a friend, at first we try to bring the friend back. When we see that it is a hopeless case, our ego comes to the fore. We say, "If he does not need us, then we also do not need him." In this way, doubt and fear leave us when we make friends with faith and courage.

> *In the inner world*
> *I can have sunshine every day,*
> *For my inner faith is founded upon*
> *God's infallible Promise-Light.*

Overcoming Doubt

The best and most effective way to conquer doubt is to feel that you are all certainty. Feel that you are all courage. Always try to identify yourself with the positive. Right now, unfortunately, you may be identifying with doubt, feeling that this is reality. But if you change your attitude, then you will say that doubt is not reality, fear is not reality; the real reality is faith, the real reality is courage. How will you do this? If doubt enters, you have to think of its antidote, which is faith. If doubt enters into your mind, immediately utter the word "faith." Just say, "I am God's child; so how can I doubt myself, how can I doubt others, how can I doubt God?"

We will never be able to conquer doubt by wishful thinking alone. We have to make a conscious effort. If we identify ourselves with the mind, we will not have the power to conquer doubt, because the mind itself unconsciously or consciously cherishes doubt. The soul has more power than the mind. We should try to save ourselves with the light of the soul. Every day, before doubt has the opportunity to enter into our mind, we should try to feel the light of the soul inside us. Each time doubt comes, we should feel that the soul is not only protecting us, but also giving us a new life—a life of constant and abundant faith, not only in God but also in ourselves.

Doubt will leave us when we feel that we are destined to do something for God. We get tremendous power from the word "destined." This word brings boundless courage to the fore. Even if somebody is weak by nature, if someone says that he is destined to work for God, then immediately, from the inner world, heroism comes forward. He will fight against any obstruction with a strength and inner determination that will surprise him.

Obstructions may come to him in the form of impurity, obscurity, jealousy, fear, and doubt, but the word "destined" will smash the pride of all the negative forces. Anything that is undivine will have to surrender to this word. So if we have the inner and outer conviction that tells us we are destined to serve God, then the goal can unmistakably be reached.

The Doubt-Monkey

When doubt or some other negative force enters into you, take it as a monkey which is constantly bothering you. You are praying and meditating, and here a monkey is bothering you. You let the monkey go on and on, because you are patient. There is a competition between your patience and the monkey's mischievous pranks. Because you are a seeker, you are bound to have more patience than someone who is not aspiring. The monkey is not aspiring, so the monkey's patience can never equal yours. We have an ego; the monkey also has a form of ego. If you are not paying any attention to it, the monkey will eventually feel that it is beneath its dignity to bother you. Patience has the capacity to dissolve wrong forces, and if you have patience, the negative forces can never win.

Doubt is an old disease.
Faith is an old medicine.
Compassion is an old doctor.
Concern is an old nurse.

Doubting God

If you doubt God, God will not lose any of His infinite capacities. You can doubt God's existence if you want to, because He is not standing right in front of you; you do not see Him or consciously feel Him. But do not doubt yourself. If somebody else has realized God, why should you not be able to do the same? The same God that exists in him also exists in you. All souls have come from the same Source, which is God. If one person has realized God through the aspiration of his soul, you can do it too.

Your doubt is baseless. Although your aspiration may not yet be as intense as the other person's aspiration was, you have to feel that God can never be fulfilled until you have realized Him. God's existence needs fulfillment in and through you. If your friend has realized God but you still remain unrealized, then rest assured that God remains unfulfilled. He will be fulfilled only on the day when all human beings have realized Him.

You may have absolute faith in God's existence, but you may doubt God's Compassion. You may say: "Is God really so compassionate? I have done so many things wrong in my life. Will He still give me His Knowledge-Light? Why should He show me His unconditional Compassion?" To conquer this kind of doubt, remember that once upon a time you were a soul in the soul's world. Who brought your soul into this world? It was God. Before you were consciously aware of spirituality, divinity, and reality, God gave you life. God gave you the message of divinity. Already you can see how much God has given you although you never consciously asked for these things. It has all come to you through your soul. Who created your soul? God. Who offered it to you? God. Who is going to fulfill you through your soul? Again, it is God. So you can easily stop doubting God's Concern.

God's business is to fulfill Himself and manifest

Himself on earth. If you consciously aspire, then it becomes easier for Him to fulfill and manifest Himself through you. If you offer Him your sincerity and your aspiration, and take one step toward Him, He will take ninety-nine steps toward you. You give what you can, and God will give you not only what He has but also what He is. What He has is infinite Concern and what He is is infinite Light.

My Lord Supreme,
What will You do for me
If I give You my heart's blossoming faith?
"My child,
I shall take away
Your mind's brooding doubts."

Faith Works Miracles

Absence of doubt is one thing, but faith, real faith, is something else. The study of books and scriptures can give us information and a certain understanding. It can give us, at most, inspiration, but nothing more. By borrowing others' ideas, we can never be truly enlightened in our inner life. It is by studying the eternal book of Truth within us, by listening constantly to the voice of the inner self, that we can become spiritually enlightened. It is then that we will find joy in our outer life. We must see God first, and then we can become godlike. If we want to be truly godlike, our talking must give way to becoming.

Let me tell you a true story. Throughout India, people pray to Lord Krishna, a great spiritual Master who lived on earth thousands of years ago. In a certain village in Bengal, India, a rich man's servant went to his master's house every day by crossing a river in a ferryboat. One day there was a violent storm. The ferry could not cross the raging river, and the servant, who was forced to go many miles out of his way to a footbridge, was late in arriving. His master was furious. "You fool," he shouted, "if you utter Lord Krishna's name three times, you will see that you do not need a boat. You will be able to walk across the river!"

That afternoon, as the storm showed no signs of abating, the poor servant was threatened with the same situation. This time, in his simple faith, he obeyed his master's instructions. From the very depths of his heart he uttered the name of Lord Krishna. Lo, the miracle of miracles! He felt a power propelling him toward the water, and he was able to walk upon the very waves. Thus he crossed the river.

When the master heard the story, his joy knew no bounds. A swelling pride rose in his heart. Was it not his advice that had brought about the success? "I never knew that my advice had such great power," he thought. "Let me enjoy this miracle myself."

The rich man went to the river, which was now calm and serene, and uttered Lord Krishna's name three times. He began to cross, but fear and doubt tortured his whole being, and although he shouted the sacred name hundreds of times, his attempt was fruitless. He drowned.

What do we learn from this story? The servant had sincere faith in his master. He also had implicit faith in Lord Krishna. It was this absolute faith in a divine power that saved him and proved the power of Lord Krishna's grace.

If something is true, you will feel it within the very depths of your heart, although sometimes it may take a little time. After a seed is sown, it takes a few months for it to germinate. In a year it grows into a sapling, and eventually it grows into a huge banyan tree.

When you begin to take an interest in the spiritual life, you have sown the seed. You may not see the results immediately. You *will* feel light and peace, but first you have to have faith. Inside your body there are many organs: the heart, lungs, and so on. You believe this because doctors and others say so. Although you cannot see these organs, you know that they are there. Similarly, in the inner world, if you do not see something right now, you cannot say that it does not exist. In your inner life there are many things which you may not be aware of right now, but if you pray and meditate soulfully, and cultivate more faith in what you have heard from spiritual seekers and Masters, then eventually you will see that they are absolutely correct.

You have to start with faith—sincere, genuine, sublime faith. This faith is not going to mislead you. When you read a spiritual book, that book embodies light. While reading, you may not feel light inside the book right away, but still you do not discard the book. You have some faith in the messages that the book contains. You meditate on the words and ideas that the book embodies, and eventually you do get light. Inside the book there is a hidden reality. If you believe in that hidden reality while you are reading, in the course of time you will get illumination. But you have to read the book in order to get the essence, the quintessence of the book.

Similarly, you have to pray and meditate before you will feel your own divinity. If you cannot feel your inner divinity right now, do not be sad or upset. Pray and meditate sincerely, and through your faith, your real divinity will one day loom large. If you do not have higher experiences or realizations as soon as you enter the spiritual life, do not give up. Right now if you do not feel inside the very depths of your heart something divine, illumining, fulfilling, and perfect, no harm. It takes time to acquire a free access to the inner world. But once you have free access to the inner world, you will see that it is flooded with light and delight.

You are crying
Because the quantity of your mind's doubts
Is as vast as the ocean.
Why do you not smile and dance,
Since you know that the quality of your heart's faith
Is as pure as a morning rose?

The Faith of a Child

You are God's child, not God's slave. If you can approach God as your Father, then you can say, "My Father is rich. My Father is great. My Father is kind. He is bound to give me a portion of His kindness, His greatness, and His wealth." This is the spontaneous feeling a child will have.

If you feel that God is the Lord and you are His slave, then how are you going to have faith in yourself? A slave will immediately say, "Today he is my master. Tomorrow he may kick me out." A slave cannot claim his master's wealth or capacity as his very own. But a child can.

If you want to have faith in yourself, first you have

to feel what kind of connection or relationship you have established with your Inner Pilot. If it is the relationship of Father and child, or Mother and child, or lover and Beloved, if it is the relationship of two most intimate, absolutely closest friends, then you can expect everything from God. But if you cannot establish that kind of sweet oneness between yourself and God, then how will you maintain any faith? If you think, "He is very aloof; He is the Lord Supreme, and I am just a meaningless creature," then there can be no feeling of oneness. If you think of yourself as a tiny ant and God as a huge elephant, naturally you will say, "Oh, how can I have any strength or capacity? I am so weak and insignificant." If you think of God as someone who is more than eager to give you what He has, then you will feel, "The strength that God has is all for me. When the time comes, He will offer it to me." When you have established that kind of feeling, when you feel that your Father is going to give you everything that you need, then automatically you will have abiding faith.

In the morning
I feed my faith-flames.
In the evening
I see something quite astonishing:
All my doubts have died
Of starvation.

The Eye of Faith

Faith is the eye that is shared by both God and man. This eye of faith sees the future inside the immediacy of the present. If we have faith in the spiritual life, we do not stumble, we do not walk, we do not march. No! We simply run! If we have implicit faith in God, in the Inner Pilot, and in our own aspiration, then we constantly run the fastest toward our destined goal.

Jesus Christ said, "Blessed are those who have believed and have not seen." People who believe only what they see with their naked eyes are eating only half the fruit. To scrutinize the Truth is to lose it. Truth is a matter of identification. This is the Christ's lofty pronouncement about faith and doubt. Blessed are those who have faith without demanding proof at every moment.

What you call faith, I call the soul's foreknowledge of the highest Truth. Faith tells us not only what God is but also what God can do for us at every moment. This faith is our living breath in God the Omniscient and God the Omnipotent.

See through the eye of faith. You will see the eternal Truth. Feel through the heart of faith. You will feel the immortal Truth.

What is sleepless faith?
It is a beacon-light for those
Who are sailing in the Golden Boat
Toward the Golden Shore.

CHAPTER FOUR

Fear-Enemy and Courage-Hero

There is no other way to please our inner self
Than to be a perfect emblem of courage.

Courage is absolutely necessary in the spiritual life. The very acceptance of the spiritual life demands enormous courage. This courage is not the courage of a haughty, rough person who will strike others to assert his superiority; it is totally different. This courage is our constant awareness of what we are entering into, of what we are going to become, of what we are going to reveal.

Fear is a negative force, a destructive force, and we are

the soldiers who will fight against it. Fear comes from darkness, from ignorance. If we enter a room that is pitch-dark, we will be frightened. But as soon as we turn on the light, the darkness is illumined and our fear vanishes.

Why Fear Exists

Fear can come into existence for various reasons, but the main reason is our sense of separateness. If I feel that you are my own, my very own, then I will not be afraid of you, no matter how strong and powerful you are. A child is not afraid of her father's strength. The father is perhaps six feet tall, stout and strong. Everybody is afraid of his physical strength, but the child goes right up to the father and plays with him. No matter how strong he is, the child is not afraid of her father because she has established an inner oneness with him. She claims her father's strength as her own.

The world around us very often frightens and threatens us. It causes unnecessary fear in our mind or in our existence. Why? Precisely because we have not yet established our oneness-reality with it. Fear looms large when our sense of separateness looms large. Fear exists just because we want to remain separated, consciously or unconsciously, from the all-pervading Reality which we eternally are.

> *Fear is a real enemy. What does it do?*
> *It buys our coffin long before we are destined to die.*

Freedom from Fear

Fear can exist in all parts of our being: our body, vital, mind, and heart. To free our body from fear, what we need is the glorious experience of our soul. To free our vital from fear, what we need is the dynamic expansion of our soul. To free our mind from fear, what we need is the transforming illumination of our soul. Finally, to free our heart from fear, what we need is the fulfilling perfection of our soul.

Most of the time we experience fear in the mind and not in the heart. The aspiring heart knows how to establish its inseparable oneness with the reality that is within and without. But the doubtful, suspicious, and sophisticated mind finds it difficult to see eye-to-eye with the reality that is blossoming right in front of us. The mind suspects the reality before it. And there even comes a time when the mind, to its wide surprise, doubts its own judgment. At that time the mind feels a tremendous sense of dissatisfaction. Once it was the judge and now it has become a victim of its own judgments. But right from the beginning, the heart tries to identify itself with the reality around it. On the strength of its identification with that reality, it absorbs what the reality is and what the reality stands for. If we live in the aspiring heart, the heart that cries for the all-pervading oneness-reality, the torture of fear can easily come to an end.

To conquer fear in the mind, one has to empty the mind daily. The mind is full of doubt, obscurity, ignorance, suspicion, and so forth. Early in the morning, for ten minutes or so, try not to have any thoughts—good or bad, divine or undivine. If a thought comes, do not let it enter. Then, after some time, allow only the divine thoughts which are your friends to enter. In the beginning you may not know which thought is your friend and which thought is your enemy, so you have to be very careful. Your friends are divine thoughts, progressive thoughts, illumined thoughts, that will undoubtedly conquer fear in the mind. Feel that your mind is like a vessel. First empty it, and then wait for peace, light, and bliss to descend. If you do not first empty the vessel, then peace, light, and bliss will not be able to enter.

> *Nothing compels you to shiver*
> *In helpless slavery.*
> *Just don your God-given*
> *Aspiration-bravery.*

Fear of Failure

To conquer the fear of failure, you have to know what failure is and what it can do. Fear is bound to disappear when you realize that failure is not something shameful, damaging, destructive, or painful, but something natural. When a child starts to walk, he often stumbles and falls down. He does not feel that stumbling is a failure. He thinks that it is a natural process to stand up for a moment and then fall down again.

If you think of failure not as something that is opposed to reality but as something that is forming and becoming reality, then there will not be any fear. We take failure as something contrary to our expectation, but failure is something that urges us forward. What we call failure, in God's Eye is only an experience. We must always take failure not as a finished product or as the culmination of an experience but, rather, as part of the process of experience.

Let us say that you have worked very hard to achieve a particular result and you fail. Instead of giving in to waves of disappointment and despair, try to see the divine purpose in your activity. Perhaps it helped you to increase your patience, wisdom, and other divine qualities. If you adopt this approach, you will be able to go beyond the crushing blows of failure.

Fear of the Inner Life

Sometimes people are afraid of spirituality itself. If they knew the real significance of spirituality, they would in no time embrace it. Spirituality shows us our goal, and that goal is the realization of the Infinite within us.

Perhaps you are afraid of the inner life. You may feel that the moment you launch into the inner life, you will be completely lost, like a babe in the woods. You may also think that in accepting the inner life you are building castles in the air. Finally, you may feel that to accept the inner life is to throw yourself into the mouth of a roaring lion that will completely devour you. You have countless sweet dreams. You want to transform these dreams into reality, and you feel that if you embark on the inner life, you will be deprived of all these achievements. Naturally, you start shying away from the inner life.

The inner light can never disappoint you. It is the night that disappoints. If you bathe in the sea of light, you will not be lost. During your meditation, and during your waking hours, try to consciously feel that you are growing into the inner light. When you grow into the inner light, your feeling of fear is bound to disappear. You came into existence from the inner light and now you are becoming more conscious of it.

If you are afraid to enter into the spiritual life wholeheartedly, try to determine whether the outer world can ever be truly satisfying. One day, after you have had a very good meditation, take a few moments to identify yourself with your friends or others who are not aspiring. Some of them may be very rich and prosperous, some may have big families, but have their lives brought them real happiness or merely frustration and sorrow? Then examine your own life. You may not have millions of dollars, but you are the happiest person. What has made you happy? Your aspiration and meditation.

The spiritual life can never be an artificial life. Spirituality is something natural and spontaneous. It tells us that we need not be bound by frustration, fear, and anxiety. It tells us that if our outer life is full of misery, frustration, defeat, and limitation, it is equally true that we have within us an ideal life which is all harmony, all perfection, all fulfillment. The inner life most gladly, cheerfully, and devotedly wants to be the living bridge between our present life and our ideal life.

If you have the sincere courage
To declare that you are totally lost,
Then God has the unreserved Compassion
To show you the way
To the Satisfaction-Goal.

Meditation is absolutely the best way to overcome fear. In meditation we identify ourselves with the Vast, with the Absolute. We are afraid of someone or something because we do not feel that particular person or thing is a part of us. But when we have established our conscious oneness with the Absolute, we feel that everything is part of us. And how can we be afraid of ourselves?

If we are afraid of someone, it is because we have not enlarged our consciousness to include them; we feel that the other person is a stranger to us. I am not afraid of any of my limbs because I claim them as my very own. When we practice spirituality, we try to enlarge our consciousness until it pervades the length and breadth of the world. With our conscious awareness, we become one, totally one, with the universe. When we become consciously one with the universe, there can be no fear.

The very purpose of meditation is to unite, expand, enlighten, and immortalize our consciousness. Most of the time, when we talk to our friends or move around, we are not consciously aware of the Divinity within us. But when we are meditating, we are consciously trying to be aware of our inmost Divinity. Divinity is not afraid of humanity because Divinity has infinite Power. When we have free access to Divinity, when our entire existence, inner and outer, is surcharged with Divinity's boundless and infinite Power, how can we be afraid of humanity? It is impossible!

> *How to conquer fear?*
> *Sit at the feet*
> *Of your illumining consciousness-light.*
> *This light has the adamantine willpower*
> *To protect you, perfect you, and liberate you.*

God the Love

Where there is love, real love, there can be no fear. Why do we fear? We fear because we have separated ourselves from God's Love and we are apt to think of God the Omnipotent, not God the All-Love. But even the omnipotent God is not a God that threatens or strikes us with an iron rod every time we make a mistake.

There is no such being as God the tyrant. There is

only one God, and that God is God the Love. This God does not punish us. This God is constantly shaping us in His own way. It is He who is the Doer, it is He who is the Action, and it is He who is the Enjoyer, both in the action and in the result. We feel that we are the doers, and that if we do something wrong God will punish us mercilessly. This is not so. It is God's Dream that each individual embodies. It is God's Reality that each individual has to manifest here on earth. It is in each human being that God's Reality lives.

Since we are praying to God the Almighty, meditating on God the Almighty, why should we be afraid of anything or anyone? A child feels his mother has all the power in the world. When he is afraid of anything, he runs to his mother because he knows that his mother has utmost affection for him. You are a spiritual child of God, so when you are attacked by any kind of fear, immediately try to run toward the sweet Supreme, who is all Compassion, all Love, all Blessings. Since you are a seeker, there should be no fear, for you are taking shelter inside the infinite Affection of the Absolute Supreme.

The Story of Gandhi Buri

Courage is the outer expression of our inner indomitable will. You can get courage from your aspiration if you can make yourself feel that you are a chosen hero-instrument of the Supreme. The very word "hero," the very concept of heroism, can grant you courage. Again, aspiration itself is courage. Only a brave person can aspire. When we have aspiration, we have inner courage. Against inner courage, death itself contends in vain.

In the time of the British rule of India, there once lived an extremely patriotic woman. She was a great admirer of the distinguished Indian leader Mahatma Gandhi; his very name was for her a sea of inspiration. Despite the fact that she was seventy-three years old, she did many patriotic things that inspired the people of India with the hope of getting the British out of the country. Because of this woman's admiration for Mahatma Gandhi, people called her Gandhi Buri, *buri* meaning "old lady."

In 1942, Mahatma Gandhi was arrested, and all of India was furious. Around the nation, people held processions and shouted the slogan "Quit India," which was

Mahatma Gandhi's message to the British government. The day after Gandhi's arrest, Gandhi Buri was involved in a march to a police station. The people in the procession wanted to pull down the British flag that was flying over the police station and hoist up the Indian flag in its place.

The police stood in the way and warned the protesters that if they came forward they would be shot. All the marchers stopped except Gandhi Buri. She snatched India's flag from one of the young boys in the procession and ran toward the building. At first the police laughed at her. "Enough!" they cried. "No more! Get out of here, old woman. We do not want to kill you."

Gandhi Buri's immediate response was "Kill me! I am not afraid. I want to free my Mother India!"

She ran toward the staircase that led to the top of the police station. Before she reached the stairs the police shot her. She was still holding the flag in her right hand as she chanted the slogan of the Indian independence movement, "*Bande Mataram, Bande Mataram, Bande Mataram*"—"Mother, I bow to thee." Then she died.

This old woman was so courageous that she gave her life for her country. From that day on, many of the people who were in that procession dedicated their lives to the freedom of India.

If we are sincere enough to go deep within and to feel that inner courage belongs to us, inner courage can dawn at every moment. When we use our adamantine will, which we can easily have at our behest, we can conquer the very breath of fear.

To rise triumphantly out of every trial, what we need is inner courage. Inner courage is the constant acceptance and fulfillment of God's Will.

CHAPTER FIVE

The Jewel of Humility

My ego talks,
My humility acts.

Humility is the real secret of the spiritual life. When we embody humility, we neither underestimate nor overestimate our life. Humility is not a matter of touching the feet of somebody. It is our feeling of consecrated oneness with humanity. Real humility is the expansion of our consciousness. It is the God-life within us. The higher we go, the greater is our promise to the Supreme in mankind. The more light we receive by virtue of our humility, the more we have to offer mankind.

When we really have something to offer, and when we want to offer it with a devoted quality, then humility automatically comes to the fore. While we are achieving something, we have to constantly remember to be humble in order to be of greater service to mankind. In self-giving we become truly happy.

In our human life when we achieve something, immediately pride, vanity, and many other forces enter into us. We extol ourselves to the skies. Or insecurity comes. No matter how powerful, how rich, or how wise we are, we do not feel totally secure. But when we practice meditation regularly and devotedly, we get abundant peace, light, and bliss. When we get these qualities, automatically we feel that it is our bounden duty to become inseparably one with the rest of the world. At that time, real humility dawns.

Big "I," Little "i"

The ego, which is the little "i," is extremely limited. It is constantly seeking something other than itself. The very nature of the ego is to be dissatisfied and displeased. It is never satisfied with what it has and what it is, because it feels that the truth is always somewhere else.

The large "I," the Self, is not seeking anything, for it embodies everything within itself. We cannot define the universal Self with our mental concepts. We can only realize it on the strength of our aspiration.

The little "i" will always make us feel that we as individuals are most important. But if we care only for our own self-perfection and ignore the rest of the world, we are totally lost. Our larger Self tells us that we belong to the Infinite, the Eternal and the Immortal. On the strength of our identification with the Absolute, we care for the full perfection of God's entire creation.

Now that you see through
Your real weakness,
Volcano-pride,
You are ready to discover
Your real strength,
Oneness-love.

Helping or Serving?

We have to be careful when we use the term "help." Let us use the word "service" instead. When we serve someone, we have humility. But when we feel that we are helping someone, pride, vanity, and ego immediately come forward. When we help, we feel that we have more capacity than someone else, and when we are being helped, we feel that we have less capacity. Inside help there is a feeling of superiority or inferiority. But when we serve soulfully, there can be no pride, because we do not feel superior. We feel that we are serving the Supreme in others. When we serve, we make the other person feel the Supreme's presence within himself. True service is rendered with humility, and it comes only with true and constant aspiration.

If we wish to live in the world and work for the world, our attitude should be one of dedicated service. We have been given a golden opportunity to serve others, and for this we should feel grateful to God.

Catching the Ego-Thief

How can we get rid of the ego? Feel that your ego is a thief inside you. When you see a thief, what do you do? You chase him. If you start chasing your ego, a day will come when you will be able to catch it. It may not happen all at once, but if you know that something is stolen and you have seen the thief, you will continue searching for the culprit. Your search is bound to be rewarded one day. When you catch the ego-thief, what will happen? You will immediately be able to transcend it. In the ego's purification and transformation is man's conscious evolution and true satisfaction.

Here is another way to conquer the ego. Suppose you are a good singer and you are very proud of your voice. Ask yourself whether you are by far the best singer on earth. Your answer will be no, for there are many who sing far better than you do. If you have studied and become a great scholar, you may feel you have every reason to be proud. But if you sincerely ask yourself whether you are the greatest scholar on earth, your immediate answer will be no. There are some people who far surpass you in knowledge and wisdom. If you think that you are really beautiful, then just ask yourself sincerely whether you are the most beautiful person in God's creation. Again the answer will be no. No matter what you are proud of, ask yourself whether there is anybody who is superior to you. You will find that there are many, many people who are far better than you in any aspect of life. Once you are aware of this fact, how can you maintain your pride?

If you want to permanently get rid of vanity, ego, and pride, dive deep into the sea of spirituality. There you will be able to discover your true self. In your self-discovery, ego, with all its limitations, cannot breathe. When peace, light, and bliss descend from above, vanity, pride, and ego disappear.

The Right Hand and the Left Hand

When you establish your oneness with others, immediately you expand your consciousness. If someone does something well, you have to feel that it is you who have done it. Others should also feel the same when you do something significant. Whenever any individual does something very well, we have to feel that it is our conscious inspiration and aspiration that have enabled that individual to achieve this success. If we always have an attitude of teamwork, then we will be able to conquer the ego.

Ego comes from separativity. How can there be any ego when we feel our true inner oneness? Where is the consciousness of "I" if, when I do something, you can claim it? Where is the consciousness of "you" if, when you do something, I can claim it? It is gone—vanished within our mutual feeling of oneness. When we identify ourselves with other human beings, at that time we feel our oneness with them and the competitive spirit disappears from our life. Then there can be no ego.

In track and field, the spectators may see an athlete put the shot very far with his right hand. Everybody has seen that he threw it with his right hand, but no one will say that he has used only the right hand and not the left. The left hand did not throw the shot. But if that hand or any other part of the body had refused to cooperate, then there would have been no coordination of the body. When throwing the shot with the right hand, a counter movement from the left hand and balance from the feet are necessary.

My little finger is a part of my body, but I think of

my body as a whole, more than I think of the little finger. When I think of the body, automatically the little finger is nourished with the necessary amount of concern just because it is one with the body as a whole. It does not separate its existence and its consciousness from the rest of the body. If the finger is cut, the whole body will suffer from the pain. When the body is nourished, the little finger maintains its strength or gains strength. It cannot be isolated. The body takes care of the little finger automatically, because of their inseparable oneness.

In the same way, the human consciousness is part of the Universal Consciousness. We should keep the Universal Consciousness before our eyes no matter what we are doing, whether we are eating or singing or working in the office. If we think of the Universal Consciousness as the whole body and our individual human consciousness as a tiny finger, then we can easily identify ourselves with the Universal Consciousness. Inside the Universal Consciousness, everything is constantly expanding and growing into higher and more fulfilling light.

I shall play with everyone
On the day I play with You.

The Wings of Joy

I shall blend in every heart
On the day I blend in You.

Human Pride and Divine Pride

Pride can exist in different forms. Somebody has done well in school and he is proud of this. Somebody has stood first in sports and he is proud of his achievement. Somebody has done something excellent, so naturally he is proud. In human pride, ego is always present. I am proud because *I* have done something, because *my* friend or *my* brother has done something. It is all *mine, mine.*

There is also something called divine pride. Divine pride comes on the strength of our oneness with God. On the strength of his highest consciousness, the Christ said, "I and my Father are one." How could he say this? His divine utterance was based on his inner realization of his inseparable oneness with God, the eternal Father. To most people, God is just a vague idea. They think that God is far away in the blue skies or somewhere other than where they are. But for the Christ, God was a living reality.

We have to know what kind of pride we are dealing

with, the pride that binds us or the pride that frees us. Human pride says, "My and mine: there the reality ends." Divine pride says, "God is mine. The Almighty, the Infinite, is mine. How can I bind myself to anything limited and limiting?" Divine pride does not bind; it frees. It is our feeling of inseparable oneness with the Infinite Vast. When our human pride comes forward, we have to remind ourselves: "I am God's chosen child. How can I do this? How can I be so mean, so selfish, so undivine? It is beneath my dignity." Divine pride is excellent; it will always help us.

A Drop and the Ocean

The common conception of security is an achievement or a possession on the physical plane. But an abiding sense of security can never come from possession or from achievement. Impossible! Even the President of the United States, who has the top position, can be blown away at any second like a trembling leaf. Security comes only when we have established our constant oneness with our soul.

If we want to become one with our soul, we must always try to be aware of our Source, which is eternal Peace, Light, and Bliss. If our Source is something divine, eternal, and infinite, how can we feel insecure? A person is insecure when he feels that darkness is all around him. At night you are frightened because there is no light. We must always be aware of the fact that the Being who is inside us and around us is all Light, and this Light is immortal. Whatever is real, divinely real, is immortal. The Reality inside us is divine and eternal. If we have something eternal within us to think of us and care for us, how can we feel insecure?

If you can become consciously and constantly aware that you are of the Source, that you came from Light and Delight and your ultimate goal is to go back to Light and Delight, then you will have no sense of insecurity. As long as the tiny drop retains its individuality and separateness, it will remain insecure; the waves and surges of the ocean will scare it to death. But when the tiny drop consciously enters into the ocean, it becomes the ocean itself. Then it is no longer afraid of anything.

Beyond speech and mind,
Into the river of ever-effulgent Light
My heart dives.
Today thousands of doors, closed for millennia,
Are opened wide.

Humility and Power

Humility is not a sign of cowardice. Soulful humility is itself a form of divine power. Humility is the soul's strength. What we call "humility" in Heaven, we call "strength" on earth. When the soul's strength manifests, it does so through humility.

Power in the physical, power in the vital, and power in the mind find it difficult to be humble. But power in the heart finds it quite easy to be humble. Power in the heart has the feeling of oneness.

How can we have power and humility at the same time? Think of the mother. The mother is much stronger and wiser than the child. But the mother does not feel that it is beneath her dignity to touch the feet of the child. She knows that she is doing it on the strength of her complete oneness with him. The mother is very tall, but when she wants to offer food to the child, she bends down. The child's love for the mother is not less just because she bends down. On the contrary, it increases considerably. The child sees that the mother is tall and could easily stay at her own height while the child struggles to grow up. But out of her kindness she does not do that. There is no superiority; there is only a feeling of oneness. Humility means oneness with the rest of the world. On the strength of our humility, we become vast. Vastness itself is power.

We must realize
That there is only one way
Of acquiring infinite possibilities.
That way lies in the greatest power:
Humility.

God Knocks Only at Humility's Heart-Door

Many years ago, a seeker came to the great Indian Master Swami Bhaskarananda at a gathering and asked him a few questions. Bhaskarananda had answered everybody else's questions, but he would not answer this seeker. Instead he insulted him and told him to go away.

Everybody was shocked at the Master's behavior, and the seeker went home very sad. But that night he had a dream, and in the dream, Swami Bhaskarananda answered his questions with utmost affection.

The next day the seeker told the others why the Master had not answered his questions in front of everyone. The others had asked their questions with utmost sincerity and humility, but he had asked his questions with tremendous pride. That is why Swami Bhaskarananda had insulted him instead of answering his questions. That night Swami Bhaskarananda had forgiven him and answered the questions in his dream. The seeker was very pleased with the answers and extremely grateful that Swami Bhaskarananda had illumined his pride.

Pride separates, humility unites. Pride is the vision of a blind man. Humility is the vision of a God-man. A Master knows that a seeker cannot receive anything if pride is what he has and what he is. Humility is receptivity in the purest sense of the term. Humility welcomes both God the Creator and God the creation in its ever-expanding life and ever-soaring heart.

True and False Humility

Humility does not mean false modesty. Humility does not mean taking a back seat. When you take a back seat consciously and deliberately in order to show others how humble you are, you are not being humble at all.

False humility is what a slave shows to his master. A slave knows that if he does not obey his master blindly, if he does not show this kind of outer humility, the master will punish him.

True humility is something totally different; it is the feeling of oneness. Humility means giving joy to others. Here on earth we want to get joy. But how do we get joy? Real joy we get from self-giving, not by possessing or by showing our own supremacy. When we allow others to get joy, then we feel that our joy is more complete, more perfect, more divine. By making others feel that they are either equally important or more important, we show our true humility.

One who knows the meaning of humility is truly divine. Humility *is* true divinity. Humility is our soul's light spreading everywhere. When the soul's light is expressed by the physical being on the strength of absolute oneness with all human beings, this is divine humility. Nothing can enter an individual so silently and at the same time so convincingly as humility.

It is through humility that we can dive the deepest and climb the highest in our meditation. In humility is oneness, and in oneness is our divine reality.

Remain unseen,
Remain unapplauded.
Faster than the fastest
You alone, and nobody else,
Will be able to run.

Nature's Humility

When you really have something to offer to the world, then you can become truly humble. A tree, when it has no fruit to offer, remains erect. But when the tree is laden with fruit, it bends down. If you are all pride and ego, then nobody will be able to get anything worthwhile from you. When you have genuine humility, it is a sign that you have something to offer mankind.

How can you become humble? You can meditate on a tree. When it offers its fruit to the world, it bows down with utmost humility. When it offers shade or protection, it offers them to everyone without regard to wealth or rank or capacity. When the tree develops flowers and fruit, the tree bends down and shares its fruits with the world.

Look at Mother-Earth, who is protecting us, nourishing us and giving us shelter in every way. How many bad things are being done to Mother-Earth! Yet she is all-forgiving. Right in front of us we can see humility in a patch of grass. When we see grass with our human eyes, we feel that it is something unimportant. Anybody can step on it. But when we see it with our inner eye, we feel how great it is. Early in the morning when we see dew on the grass, we say, "How beautiful it looks!" A few hours later we may be walking on it; yet it never complains or revolts. If we walk gently on the grass, we can get the sense of oneness with Mother-Earth. When we have the inner capacity to appreciate the grass, we say, "How humble and self-giving it is!"

Like the tree I shall bow down.
Like the mountain I shall forgive and keep my head high.
Like the mother I shall always remain awake.
Like the heart I shall always worship.

CHAPTER SIX

Moving from Worry to Confidence

A confidence-heart and an assurance-mind are undoubtedly
Two immortal boons from above to humanity.

Worries—mental, vital, and physical—do exist. But it is up to us whether to accept them or reject them. If we carry our worries inside us, that means we are carrying extra weight and diminishing our capacity. The proper approach is to make the mind calm, quiet, and tranquil always. If we can have peace of mind, then we can run the fastest toward the goal.

Let God Be Responsible

Let us be practical. Do you get any benefit by worrying? No! You only torture yourself. For instance, there are many parents who worry about their children. It is natural for you to think of your children with concern, but if you go on worrying day in and day out, this worry itself becomes an undivine force in your life.

You should convince yourself that only a few years ago your children did not exist in your life. They are like flowers that you have plucked from a tree. You will not keep them forever. We can claim only those things that stay with us permanently. You should feel that you have given them to the Supreme, and He has taken responsibility for their lives. In this way, you can convince yourself not to worry about them. You are 100 percent responsible for offering goodwill to your children, who are nearest and dearest to your heart. But to worry does not help at all.

We worry because we do not know what is going to happen to us tomorrow, or even the next minute. But we have to feel that not only does God know what is best for us, He will do what is best for us at His choice Hour.

When we can feel that we are the instruments and He is the Doer, then we will not worry.

You can transform
The hurtful pressures of your life
Into delightful pleasures
Just by telling yourself
That the world around you can easily exist
And even prosper
Without you.

Making Friends with Time

The soul knows that there is an eternal Time, and the soul is constantly growing in the eternal Time. Unfortunately, when we remain in the physical mind or physical consciousness, it is simply impossible for us to think of something immortal or eternal. We limit ourselves to earthbound time. Earthbound time is broken up into fragments: one minute, two minutes, three minutes. We feel that we are constantly fighting against time in order to accomplish the things that we have to do. That is why our minds become agitated and stricken with worries. But when we pray and meditate, we do not break up time in this way. Instead, at a glance we see the infinite and eternal Time, which is a smooth, unbroken flow, and we enter into eternal Time.

The first and foremost thing is to have peace of mind. When you have established peace of mind, then you will see that the things you are trying to achieve will be easily accomplished. A runner knows that if he carries extra weight, his opponents will defeat him. When doubt, fear, insecurity, or any other negative forces enter into your mind, just empty them out. When the mind is calm and tranquil, then you can run the fastest.

Always regard time as a great friend of yours. We can become more aware of the value of time by realizing that each moment is a golden opportunity given by God. If we avail ourselves of each opportunity devotedly and wisely, then we will run the fastest toward our destined goal.

Because I am a truth-seeker,
The future flows toward me.
Because I am a God-lover,
I live in the eternal Now.

The Wings of Joy

There is a great difference between anxiety and alertness. They are two different dynamic energies. With anxiety, you are always worrying about others, comparing yourself to them, or wondering whether you can meet their expectations. But with alertness, you simply want to do the best you can.

There are quite a few things you can do when anxiety strikes. For example, if you are running a race, try to feel that you are the only runner in the race. Before the gun goes off, do not think of others. Think only that you are going to run at your own fastest speed. In this way there can be no anxiety.

If you are performing for an audience, feel that there is only one person listening to you, and imagine that that person is a child of only two years. This is the human way to overcome your anxiety. The divine way is to imagine the Supreme right in front of you. If you see the Supreme and feel that you are also the Supreme, then how can one Supreme be afraid of the other Supreme? There is only one Supreme. If you bow down to the Supreme inside each individual in the audience, then immediately you will become one with each individual and you will not be afraid.

You can get rid of anxiety for a short time by ignoring it, but if you want to get rid of it permanently, you have to bring light into it. In the beginning, if you can convince your mind that anxiety does not exist, then you will get temporary relief. If even for one day you are freed from anxiety, you will have accomplished something. But until you have illumined anxiety, there can be no real satisfaction. You can illumine anxiety by consciously bringing light into your system through prayer and meditation.

No more brooding,
No more despondency.
Your life shall become
The beauty of a rose,
The song of the dawn,
The dance of the twilight.

A Cure for Worry

When we are assailed by worries and anxieties, the best cure is to inwardly feel God's Love for us. Worries and anxieties will go away only when we identify ourselves with something that has peace, poise, divinity, and the feeling of absolute oneness. If we identify ourselves with our Inner Pilot, then we get the strength of His illumining Light. Worries come because we identify ourselves with fear. By worrying all the time or by thinking negative thoughts, we will never move toward our goal. We will enter into divinity only by having positive thoughts: "I am of God. I am for God." If we think this, then there can be no worry, no anxiety.

Let us consciously offer our very existence—what we have and what we are—to God. What we have is aspiration to grow into the very image of God, into infinite peace, light, and bliss. What we are right now is just ignorance, the ignorance-sea. If we can offer our aspiration-cry and our ignorance-sea to God, then our problem is solved. We will not worry about our destiny, for we will know and feel that it is in the all-loving hands of God.

God is the eternal Life-Tree; we are His projecting

branches. Right now we are not aware of our own reality. We are not aware that we are part and parcel of the Life-Tree which is God. Therefore, we are insecure. But by praying and meditating we come to realize that the branches, leaves, and flowers are part of the Tree itself. When we realize this, we become secure in the Source and secure in the flow.

If I can always have
A childlike confidence,
Then my Lord Supreme
Will, without fail, become
My sleeplessly self-sacrificing Friend.

Dealing with Criticism

How can you stop worrying about what people think of you? First of all, you have to know who is dearest to you in this world—God is the dearest. You have to feel that if He is displeased with you, then you have to pay attention, because you do not want to hurt your dearest. But if the world is displeased with you or speaks ill of you, then let the world play its role. If the world is going to bark at you like a dog, that does not mean you have to bark back.

If you can feel that God is your only existence, God will give you a sea of tranquillity, a sea of inner peace. There you will see that the criticism of the rest of the world appears as a tiny bubble. The play of the bubble will end when it enters into the sea of your own vast consciousness-light.

The Critic Within

You have two voices inside you. One encourages you, "Go forward, march on! You are doing the right thing." The other one discourages you. It says that you have to become much better, because right now you are imperfect in every way.

The voice that encourages you is your conscience, your inner being, telling you that you are doing the right thing. It is like a mother encouraging her child. The child is trying to do something and the mother says, "Come, my child, you are doing well. Continue. Go as fast as you can." This encouragement and inspiration give the child a tremendous push forward.

The other voice inside you is constantly making you feel miserable by telling you that you are doing everything wrong. It is always pointing out defects and imperfections in your nature. Do not think that that voice is telling you the truth. No, it is only trying to discourage you by throwing cold water on your efforts and destroying your self-confidence while it pretends to be impartial. By telling you constantly that what you are doing, saying, and feeling is wrong, it is not helping you in any way to go faster toward your goal. On the contrary, if you have just a little possibility, the critic within you is killing it. So feel that the voice that is encouraging you is the divine voice, and the one that is discouraging you is the undivine voice in you.

To overcome self-criticism, take it as a thorn that has entered into you. The voice that is discouraging has made you feel that all the bad qualities of the world are inside you. You see yourself as very undivine. When one thorn has entered into you, you have to take the help of another thorn to remove it. That thorn is to repeat: "I am God's child, God's chosen child, and I am going to be His perfect instrument. There is nothing on earth that can prevent me from becoming His chosen instrument." You can use this thorn to take out the other thorn that is causing you trouble. Self-criticism can only be conquered by proper self-appreciation.

You have to claim the right person as your own. God is your Source. Right now you are not aware twenty-four hours a day, but a day will come when you will be aware all the time that you are God's chosen child. You are here on earth to serve Him, to fulfill Him.

The Seeds of the Future

We can have more joy and less tension in our daily life only through self-giving, not by demanding. When there is tension, it is because we want something to be done in our own way while others want it done in their way. Tension starts in the mind because we see light in one way and others see light in some other way. Tension also comes when we want to do something in the twinkling of an eye that takes two hours or two days to do. Perhaps God wants us to take two hours or two days to achieve our goal. If we can keep God's Hour in mind and not our own hour, we will get joy. Tension goes away from our mind when we know the art of surrendering to God's Will.

> You have given freedom to your mind.
> Therefore, your mind causes worries for you
> About the future.
> Why do you not give freedom to your heart?
> Your heart will definitely prepare you
> For the future.

Real Confidence and False Confidence

Divine confidence says, "I can do this because God is within me. Otherwise I could not do it. I only mix with wisdom, light, and delight because my Source is God." If a child knows that his parents are rich, he is confident. When we feel that God, who is our Mother and Father, has infinite spiritual wealth, we have real confidence; we have peace of mind. Real confidence we get when we see the Source within us.

Human confidence is no confidence at all. We say that we have confidence, but we know within ourselves that we are just showing off. When we are sincere, we realize that we are trying to fool others. When we have divine confidence, we are not fooling anybody, because we know that our Source is the Supreme, who has everything. That is why we are confident. When we become one with Him, we know He will supply us with all His wealth in infinite measure.

The Cyclone

Once a middle-class couple from Calcutta was traveling to Europe on a large ship. After a few days, a cyclone came up suddenly and it began raining heavily. Many small boats capsized. The passengers in the large vessel raised a hue and cry because there was no way their lives could be saved from imminent catastrophe.

The wife said to her husband: "Everyone is crying because we know our lives can be counted in minutes.

Why are you so calm and quiet? Do you not have any worries or anxieties? Do you not think that we will die in a few minutes? Why are you silent?"

On hearing this, the man took a pistol from his pocket and aimed it at his wife. The wife said, "Are you crazy? What are you doing? This is no time to make jokes."

The husband smiled broadly and said, "Look, you know that it is I, your husband, your dearest one, aiming this pistol at you. You know perfectly well that I will not kill you because of my tremendous love for you. God, who is the Author of all Good, is infinitely more compassionate than I am or than I ever could be, and we are His children. Do you think that He will allow us to be destroyed, or that He will destroy us? If I cannot kill you because of the little love that I have for you, how can God destroy us? He has infinite Love for His children, although we do not know and will never know how His Love and Compassion work in and through us. May God's Will be fulfilled in God's own way. Today let us be observers, and tomorrow let us participate in the fulfillment of His Cosmic Will."

Immediately the cyclone stopped and everything became calm and quiet. The wife was so proud of her husband's wisdom.

The Mother's Possessions

The heart is the mother—the mother of love, affection, light, patience, and forgiveness. Once we truly feel that the heart embodies all these divine qualities, then we will be able to bring the confidence of the heart into the mind very swiftly, effectively, and fruitfully.

We must feel that the mind is a restless child, without wisdom and maturity, and that the heart is the mother who embodies all divine qualities. Naturally, whatever the mother has, the child can claim because the mother is ready to give whatever she has to the child. So when we think of the heart, we have to think of the Divine Mother, whose boundless qualities enter into the child while she instructs him. Then, automatically, like the flowing of a river, the heart's confidence will enter into the mind.

If we feel secure
In the depths of our heart,
We shall not challenge anybody,
For inner confidence
Is nothing short of
Complete satisfaction.

CHAPTER SEVEN

The Power of Love

When the power of love
Replaces the love of power,
Man will have a new name: God.

Love is a pure and radiant flame. When we follow the path of love, we find our spiritual life, our inner life, most fulfilling. Nothing can be greater than love. Love is life, and life itself is spontaneous nectar and delight.

If love means possessing someone or something, then that is not real love; that is not pure love. If love means giving and becoming one with everything, with humanity and Divinity, then that is real love. Real love is our total oneness with the object loved and with the possessor of love. Who is the possessor of love? God.

Whom are we loving? We are loving the Supreme in each individual. When we love the body, we bind ourselves; when we love the soul, we free ourselves. It is the soul in the individual, the Supreme in each human being, that we have to love.

You can consciously give pure love to others if you feel that you are giving a portion of your life-breath when you talk to them or think of them. This life-breath you are offering just because you feel that you and the rest of the world are totally and inseparably one. Where there is oneness, it is all pure love.

The Path of the Heart

Divine love is the quickest way to realize the Highest. The mind has played its role. Now the world is crying for the wealth of the heart, which is love. If we follow the path of the heart, we will see that deep within the heart the soul abides. True, the light of the soul permeates the whole body, but there is a specific place where the soul resides most of the time, and that is in the heart. The spiritual heart is located in the center of the chest. If we want to establish a free access to our soul, we have to focus our attention, our concentration, on the heart. This is the center of pure love and oneness.

You can reach the spiritual heart through concentration and meditation. If you want to do this, every day for a few minutes you should concentrate on the heart and nowhere else. You have to feel that you do not have a head, you do not have legs, you do not have arms; you have only the heart. When you stay in the mind, life can seem like a dry piece of wood. But when you stay in the heart, life can be turned into a sea of pure love and bliss. If you can keep your consciousness in the heart, you will gradually begin to experience a spontaneous feeling of oneness. When you cultivate the spiritual soil of the heart, you will find growing there spontaneous love for God and spontaneous oneness with God's creation.

Ramesh and Gopal

Once there was a young boy named Ramesh, who was a very good student. His parents were not only rich, but also extremely kind.

At school, the students used to bring food from home to eat during lunch hour. One day Ramesh realized that his friend Gopal had not eaten anything for lunch for a few days. Ramesh went to his friend and asked why he had not brought anything to eat with him. Gopal said, "My mother could not give me anything. She said we had nothing at home."

Ramesh said, "Do not worry. I will share with you."

"No, I cannot take your food," replied Gopal.

"Of course you can," insisted Ramesh. "My parents give me much more food than I need." Finally, Gopal agreed, and for a few weeks the two boys shared Ramesh's lunch.

One day, Gopal stopped coming to school. Ramesh was concerned. When he asked the teacher why his friend was not coming anymore, the teacher told him, "He comes from a poor family. His parents cannot afford to pay the school fees. Therefore, he can no longer come to school."

Ramesh felt sad for his friend. When school was over, he took down Gopal's address from his teacher and went to Gopal's house. Ramesh begged his friend to come back to school, saying that he would ask his parents to pay the fee. Gopal's parents were deeply moved by his kindness, and Gopal again started going to school.

Gopal's father was an old man. In a few years' time, he died. The family became totally poverty-stricken, and Ramesh supported them with his own money. When Gopal's sister was stricken with a serious disease, the family could not afford the hospital bills. Again Ramesh helped them out. In every way he was the friend and guardian of Gopal's family.

Both Ramesh and Gopal completed high school and went to college. One day Gopal said to Ramesh, "To say that my heart is all gratitude to you is an understatement. I love you more than I love my own life."

Ramesh answered him, "My friend, if you love me, that is more than enough for me. You do not have to love me more than your own life."

The Power of Love

Gopal said, "But I do, and I want to prove it." Then he opened his penknife and cut his own arm. Naturally, he began bleeding. Gopal placed a few drops of blood at the feet of Ramesh.

Ramesh cried, "What are you doing, what are you doing?" He touched the cut on Gopal's arm and placed a few drops of blood on his own heart, saying: "This is the right place for your life-blood. I give you my earthly treasure in the form of material wealth. You give me your heart's love, which is Heavenly wealth beyond all measure."

A moment's love
Can and shall
Make the world perfect.

The Heart of a Lover

It is quite easy for one human being to love another if he sees the divine in the other person. It is always advisable to go to the root, which is God. If we want to love someone, the best thing is for us to love the One who is all

Love. If we know how to love Him in Himself, then it becomes extremely easy to love Him in a human being.

When you see that a person's defects and bad qualities are obvious, try to feel that they do not represent him totally. His real self is infinitely better than what you see now. Try to see the divine in others in spite of their limitations.

By seeing someone's limitations, we do not help the other person in any way. We only delay our own progress. If we find fault with somebody, his undivine qualities are not going to disappear, nor are ours going to decrease. On the contrary, his undivine qualities will come to the fore in his defense, and our pride, arrogance, and feeling of superiority will also come to the fore. But by seeing the divine in someone, we expedite our progress and help the other person to establish his own life of reality on a divine foundation. We have to see others with the heart of a lover and not with the eye of a critic.

To see the divine in others, we have to love. It is truly said that where love is thick, faults are thin. If you really love someone, then it is difficult to find fault with him. Love means oneness. A mother, in spite of knowing her child's countless limitations, does not stop loving him, because she has established her oneness with him. If there is imperfection in the child, the mother claims this imperfection as her very own.

If you find it difficult to love the human in someone, then love the divine in him. The divine in him is God. God exists in that person just as God exists in you. To love God is extremely easy because God is divine and perfect. Each time you look at an individual, if you can consciously become aware of God's existence in him, then you will not be disturbed by his imperfections or limitations.

My Lord,
Do teach me only one thing:
How to love the world
The way You love me.

The Peace-Weapon

Anger is a great obstacle. The after-effects of anger are frustration and depression. If we allow anger, the thief, to enter into us, then it will steal our love, which is our inner treasure. When anger assails us, we must cry inwardly for deep aspiration to come to the fore and chase it away. We have to call our aspiration-police to save our most precious love-treasure.

When you become angry, it means that you have lost your oneness with the world around you. If you have oneness, then when you see imperfection, you will try to perfect it; when you see impurity, you will try to purify it. But when oneness is lacking, and you see imperfection or impurity, then you are bound to become angry.

If it is real anger, uncontrollable anger, then at that time ignorance has attacked you most powerfully. If anger is coming from outside, try to feel that an enemy is entering into you. If it is from within that anger is coming, then feel that you have allowed an enemy to live with you and now you have to try to conquer it. How? With peace.

When we meditate, our mind is inundated with peace, and when we have peace of mind, we are in a position to conquer our anger. If every day you can meditate for ten or fifteen minutes on peace, you will see that whenever somebody does something wrong to you, immediately your peace will be able to swallow it. You may have every right to be angry with someone, but you know that by getting angry with him you will only lose your precious peace of mind.

> *When my peace-heart dreams,*
> *My bliss-life sings.*

Forgive and Forget

When you are angry, first ask yourself if you are doing the right thing by becoming upset. If somebody has done a terrible thing, can you change his nature by scolding him, by insulting him, by punishing him? Impossible! Suppose somebody has done something wrong and you have scolded that person. He is extremely sorry and sheds bitter tears. If you go deep within, you will feel sorry that now that person is sad and miserable. If you are sincere, you will see that you have done many, many things worse than the person whom you have scolded. You may even start shedding tears or feeling remorse for the many thousands of things you have done wrong in your life. Like this, the misery never ends. The best thing is not to get upset. Just feel that it is an experience you had for only a few seconds.

You may forget your anger temporarily, but if you have not illumined it, then it may still pull you down. Let us say you have an unpleasant experience during the day. A few hours elapse and then you forget the experience. Unless you have forgiven the person involved, you have not illumined the anger. Anger may still be pulling you down several rungs of your consciousness-ladder. Sometimes you quarrel with the members of your family and then you go to sleep. The next morning you find that you cannot meditate. You have totally forgotten the incident, but while you were sleeping, the strength of the anger increased. When something has gone wrong, it is better to rectify it and illumine it immediately.

There are two ways to illumine anger. One way is to enlarge your heart. If you have been wronged, use your power of identification. Feel that it is you yourself, or an extended part of your own consciousness, that has done the wrong thing. The sooner you can rid yourself of the idea that somebody else has done something to you, the better off you will be.

The second way is to think of perfecting yourself. When you stop thinking of perfecting others and only care for your own aspiration, you will be liberated from anger. Instead of looking around to see who is obstructing you or standing in your way, just pay all attention to your own self-discovery. When you have discovered your true self, you will see that there is nobody imperfect on earth. Everybody is perfect in you.

Yesterday I was clever.
That is why I wanted to change the world.
Today I am wise.
That is why I am changing myself.

When Others Are Angry

When others attack you with the negative power of anger, you can resort to an infinitely superior power—the Supreme's Compassion. If you invoke the Compassion of the Supreme, which is infinitely more powerful than human anger, then you will be able to inundate the other person with that Compassion. This is the only approach that will bring abiding satisfaction.

If you cannot invoke the highest power, then you have to take the second-best course, which is the human approach. Remain indifferent. Your power of indifference can create a solid wall that anger cannot penetrate. If somebody is angry with you, just feel that you have nothing to do with that person, and he has nothing to do with you. Feel that your world is totally different from his. In this way, you will remain in your indifference-world and the other person will remain in his anger-world.

However, you may not be able to remain indifferent for long. Your own aggressive power may come forward: "If he can strike me, then I also can strike him." But if somebody has attacked you, your attitude should be different. He may have attacked you to destroy you, but you can respond in order to transform him. If someone is angry, it means he is lacking in peace; peace-money he needs badly. If you have more than you need, if you are generous, you can easily give him some of your inner wealth. But if you have only a limited amount of peace, how can you give it to others? You must keep for yourself the amount that you need. First you have to increase the amount of peace in your own life. Then you can easily share this inner wealth with a person who is angry. But when you give peace to others, you have to do it secretly. If you tell someone outwardly that he needs peace, he may become furious. Secretly, like a divine thief, enter into his heart and mind and offer him peace.

Hatred: Love in Disguise

Hate is a disguised form of love. You can only hate someone whom you really wish to love, because if you were totally indifferent to that person, you could not even get up enough energy to hate him. You may feel that in this world some people are very bad. But by feeling that a person is bad or by hating that person, are you gaining anything? On the contrary, by hating that person, you will lose something very sweet in yourself. Why should you lose something very precious of your own, just because you want to correct someone by hating him? We have to be wise. You may say that he is very bad and that you have to do something. But hate is not the right weapon to use.

If you want to use the right weapon, the most effective weapon, then you must bring forward your love.

You may think that love is not a strong weapon, whereas hatred is like a sharp knife. No. Love is infinitely more powerful than hatred. When you love someone, his divine qualities have to come forward. If someone has done something nasty to you, immediately you want to punish him and strike him. After striking him, what will happen? In you, there is something called a conscience. That conscience will prick you. You will say, "What have I done? He has done something wrong, true, but now I have done something wrong too. In which way am I superior to him?"

Loving Humanity

If you really want to love humanity, then you have to love humanity as it is now. If humanity had to become perfect before it could be accepted by you, then it would not need your love, affection, and concern. But right now, in its imperfect state of consciousness, humanity *does* need your love. You are God's creation; so is humanity. You can and must love it, for unless and until humanity has realized its supreme Goal, your own divine perfection will not be complete. Humanity is only an expression of your universal heart.

You must regard the persons around you as limbs of your own body. Without them you are incomplete. You may feel that some are less developed or less important, but each one has his role to play. God has created five fingers. Although some are shorter or weaker than others, you know that only when you have five fingers are you perfect. Your middle finger is the tallest. If you feel that for this reason you do not need your shorter fingers, then you are sadly mistaken. If you want to play the piano or type, then you need all five fingers.

You can love the people around you only when you feel the necessity of world-perfection and world-transformation. If you remain isolated as an individual, then the perfection that you achieve will be very limited. Unlimited perfection will dawn only when we love humanity as a whole. It is only by accepting humanity as part of our own life, and by helping to perfect humanity with our own illumination, that we can fulfill ourselves.

Be universal in your love.
You will see the universe
To be the picture of your own being.

Loving Yourself

If we love ourselves in an emotional or egotistical way, then we are limiting and binding ourselves. We must love ourselves just because God is breathing inside us, because God wants to fulfill Himself in and through us. We must love ourselves just because our existence and God's Reality are one and the same thing.

In the process of evolution, we are continually making progress. Slowly and steadily, we are freeing ourselves from anger, doubt, and other undivine qualities that obstruct our path. Just because we have shortcomings today, we cannot say that these undivine forces will never leave us. We have to look back into the past and see how many hours a day we lived in ignorance-life, and how many hours a day we now live in aspiration-life. If we do this, then we will definitely see that we are progressing.

When the real, the highest, the most illumined part in us comes to the fore, at that time we really love ourselves in a divine way. We love ourselves because we know who we eternally are. Today we are God the aspiration. Tomorrow, on the strength of our faith in our inner divinity, we shall become God the realization.

If you want to understand yourself,
Then do not examine yourself.
Just love yourself more sincerely,
More soulfully
And more self-givingly.

A Life of Love

Life is nothing but the expansion of love. We can cultivate divine love by entering into the Source. The Source is God, who is all Love. We must try to love all of humanity with the inner awareness, consciousness, and conviction that inside each individual is the living presence of God.

You can increase your capacity to accept love by giving love to others. The more you give, the more you receive. Self-expansion is God-expansion. You are expanding your own reality inside God's Universal Reality.

You can be more receptive to divine love if you can feel every day that your Source is all Love, and that you are on earth to offer constantly, in thought and in action, the love that you already have. At every moment you have many thoughts, so you can offer love through each of your thoughts. And each time you do something, you can feel that this action is nothing but an expression of love. While thinking and while acting, if you can feel that you are offering love to mankind, to the rest of the world, then you can be more receptive to the universal Love.

Love is the transforming power in our human nature. Love transforms our life of stark bondage into the life of mightiest freedom. Love cries for life. Love fights for life. And, finally, love grows into the Life Eternal.

Man is by nature a lover.
Only he has yet to discover the real thing to love.
This quest awakens him to the fulfillment of his real Self.

CHAPTER EIGHT

From Jealousy-Fever to Oneness-Heart

Jealousy,
You are my mind's purity-stealer,
You are my heart's peace-intruder,
You are my life's divinity-invader!

In the ordinary human life, jealousy is common. We are not conscious of the fact that jealousy can ruin all our possibilities and destroy all our inner potentialities. Therefore, we do not try to transcend or conquer jealousy.

We are jealous of people because they have certain capacities or they have achieved things that we have not been able to accomplish. But let us see how far jealousy can take us. Jealousy can never expand our consciousness. On the contrary, along with jealousy we see that limitation enters into us. When limitation enters into us, imperfection, its friend, comes with it. Imperfection is always followed by destruction. When we become jealous of others, we open the door for these three brothers— limitation, imperfection, and destruction—to come in one after the other.

Akbar's Clever Minister

This is a traditional Indian story about jealousy. The great Mughal Emperor Akbar had a minister who was also the court jester. His name was Birbal. Once for amusement Akbar asked Birbal: "How is it that there is no hair on my palm? There is hair everywhere else on my body. How is it that there is none on the palm of my hand?"

Birbal immediately answered: "It is because you always have plenty of money in your hand, and you give it away. Your palms are being rubbed constantly, so the hair there has all been rubbed away."

From Jealousy-Fever to Oneness-Heart

"But how is that you do not have hair on your palms either?" Akbar asked.

Birbal cleverly replied: "Just because I constantly receive money from you, my palms are being rubbed. You are constantly giving me money, I am constantly receiving it, and that is why we have no hair on our palms."

"But what about those who do not get money from me the way you do? Why do they not have hair on their palms?"

"Oh, that is because they are very jealous. Jealous people are always thinking of the money that you are giving me and that I am receiving from you. They constantly rub their hands together in anticipation of also receiving some money. They are always burning with jealousy and greed, and so they just rub and rub their palms together. That is why they do not have any hair on their palms either."

Akbar was highly amused and pleased; but those who were listening to Birbal were terribly embarrassed at his accusation, and they bowed their heads in shame.

By becoming jealous of what the giver has or of what the receiver gets, one can never have joy or peace of mind. When we are threatened by jealousy or other negative forces, we have to feel that we have the strongest friend within us, and that friend is the soul. Let us take shelter under the wings of the soul. Let us invoke the soul and pray for its guidance. If we call on this friend, naturally our soul will fight against the negative forces on our behalf; the soul will save us, protect us, illumine us, and perfect us.

Jealousy, Admiration, or Competition?

What is the difference between jealousy and admiration? In sincere admiration, you have the feeling of an ideal in your life. Perhaps you cannot do what some other person has done, but you admire him and his action. That means that you have a spontaneous eagerness to achieve or grow into the very thing that he has achieved. This kind of sincere admiration is not a sign of inferiority. Rather it is often a sign of the reciprocal recognition of two souls.

Jealousy is something altogether different. If you are jealous of someone's achievement, you will feel that you are ready to stab that person if you are given the chance. You may try to hide your jealousy because you feel that either in the inner world or in the outer world you will be caught red-handed. But the very presence of jealousy inside you is extremely harmful.

Sometimes jealousy comes from a feeling of competition. We want to surpass the achievements of others. But let us not compete with others to show our supremacy. Instead, let us think of the necessity for our progress. Let us only try to transcend our own capacities. What is of paramount importance is our attitude as an individual. We have to feel that we are transcending our capacities not for our own glory but in order to increase the capacity and improve the standard of the world. Then, with a devoted and soulful heart, we should offer our achievements to God, who is the Source.

Conquering Jealousy

There are many practical ways to conquer jealousy. The ordinary human way is to say to oneself, "I can sing far better than that person, but I do not sing because I do not want to waste my time." This is a clever way of making yourself feel that you are better than the other person. The spiritual way to conquer jealousy is to feel that you are one with the person who is the object of your jealousy. For example, if someone is a better actor than you are, feel that it is you who are acting. In this way, you can conquer jealousy and, at the same time, expand your own consciousness.

Once our jealousy is gone, immediately we will feel that the person we were jealous of is now a perfect friend. We will feel kindness and love for him or her. Finally, we will feel relieved that the painful jealousy-arrow has been removed from our system.

When we establish our oneness with the Source, which is God, then we cannot be jealous of anybody. If we feel that our reality is God, then each individual is like a limb of our conscious, dedicated, devoted spiritual body. If they are all limbs of my body, then they are part of my existence. How can I be jealous of them? If we establish inseparable oneness with the Source, the problem of jealousy will easily be solved.

You will be able to conquer your jealousy by loving God more. You may be jealous of someone because he is a great photographer. Again, he may be jealous of you because you are a great reporter. This kind of jealousy will never end. But there is a third party who is responsible for both of you, and that is God. If you love God and become one with Him, then you will be able to identify yourself with the capacity of others. If you become one with the Source of the capacity, then the question of jealousy does not arise. If you really want to conquer jealousy, then love the One who has given all capacities to you and to everyone.

> *Jealousy-bite*
> *Is a sickness.*
> *Its perfect and guaranteed medicine*
> *Is oneness bold.*

You Only Hurt Yourself

If we spend our time cherishing negative thoughts about someone—jealousy, doubt, or anger—then, in effect, we are making that person our master. We should be very careful of how much time we spend in thinking of others and how much time we spend in thinking of the Supreme. If we waste time thinking of others with our doubt, jealousy, anger, and other negative forces, then our own progress will be delayed.

The Wings of Joy

If we want to make fast progress, we should not criticize anybody or speak ill of anybody. We have enough problems of our own. When we criticize someone, we bring forward the problems that are being shouldered by him. Let us not criticize; let us strive only for our own perfection. We shall be responsible for ourselves and let others be responsible for themselves. In this way, each one will have ample freedom to reach his goal.

> Your mind's jealousy-dagger
> Has severely wounded you.
> If you want to be healed,
> Try to discover as soon as possible
> The flames of your aspiration-heart.

The Meditation-Medicine

It is not the actual feeling of fear or doubt or jealousy which makes us miserable, but the aftereffects, when we become conscious of what we have done. Since we have suffered the aftereffects many times, we should immediately take action to cure ourselves. In India, when people suffer from malaria, the doctors prescribe quinine. Quinine is very bitter. When you cherish jealousy, at that time meditation is like quinine, very bitter and dry. But if you know that this meditation-medicine will cure you of your fever of doubt, fear, and jealousy, the best thing is to take it.

Before you start meditating, say four things: "Fear, get out of my life! Doubt, get out of my life! Jealousy, get out of my life! Insecurity, get out of my life! I do not need you and I will never need you." Then they will all come out of you and ask, "Whom do you want?" You will reply, "I want only meditation; I want only God. The proof is that I can live without you, but you cannot live without me. Fear, you cannot live without me; that is why you come and take shelter in my body. Jealousy, you cannot live without me; that is why you come and take shelter in my vital. Doubt, you cannot live without me; that is why you come and take shelter in my mind. Insecurity, you cannot live without me; that is why you come and take shelter in my heart." When you challenge these four in a divine way, they will say it is beneath their dignity to remain inside you. "If you can live without us, how is it that we cannot live without you?" they ask, and then they go away. At that time you will have your perfect meditation.

The Wings of Joy

You want to conquer
The perpetual fever of jealousy?
I will tell you a great secret:
Just love and become one
With your oneness-heart.

from Jealousy-Fever to Oneness-Heart

CHAPTER NINE

Two Swift Runners— Cheerfulness and Enthusiasm

Remain cheerful,
For nothing destructive can pierce through
The solid wall of cheerfulness.

In the life-game, each soul consciously or unconsciously runs toward the goal of inner perfection. Naturally, you want to get there as soon as possible. To do so, you have to simplify your outer life—your life of confusion, desire, anxiety, and worry. At the same time, you have to intensify your inner life—your life of aspiration, dedication, and illumination.

When we start our meditation-journey early in the

morning, we should feel that we are continuing yesterday's journey. The next day, we should feel that we have traveled still another mile. We know that one day we will reach our goal. Even if our speed decreases, we have to continue running. When we reach the goal, we will see that it was worth the struggle.

The Importance of Action

If you think that you must withdraw from the outer life in order to achieve peace, then you are making a serious mistake. In withdrawal, our satisfaction will never dawn. In activity, we progress and achieve. In action, creation, and manifestation, we are satisfied.

Let us look at a river. The river flows constantly toward the sea. It carries all kinds of rubbish—dirt, stones, leaves, sand—that it picks up as it moves toward its goal, but it always continues flowing. We should also think of our lives as rivers running toward the sea of fulfillment. If we are afraid to act because we do not want to get involved with the imperfections of the outer world, we will never reach the goal.

We have to act. If we withdraw from life, then we are consciously and deliberately telling God that we do not want to be players in His Game. But if we expect a particular result from our action, peace will never come into our lives. We will be frustrated when the result does not meet with our expectations. We will feel that we have failed. When this happens, naturally there can be no peace.

We have to feel that action itself is a great blessing, but the result of our action we have to take as an experience. According to our own limited understanding, we will see the result as either failure or success. But in God's Eye, failure and success are both just experiences that help to develop our consciousness. Whatever happens, we should see the result of our action as the experience that God wanted to give us. Today, He may give us the experience of failure. Tomorrow, He may give us another experience that will satisfy us outwardly. No matter what result comes to us from our action, we should try to be satisfied.

To make the fastest progress,
Be an absolutely cheerful

Hero-warrior
And take both victory and failure
As parallel experience-rivers
Leading to the sea
Of progress-delight.

Feeling the Presence of God

Whenever we work, we can and should feel that we are working for God. Right now you may see your outer work as just work. But if you can see work as an opportunity to express your divine capacity or to reveal your goodness, then most certainly you are working for God at that time. When you consciously feel that you are working for God, you are moving toward your goal of perfection.

In all your activities, try to feel the presence of God. For example, while you feed your child, feel that you are feeding the God within him. While you talk to someone at the office, feel that you are talking to the divinity within him.

Enthusiasm

It is always good to have enthusiasm in our life. Without it, there is no progress. But if we are overeager, we will be trying to get things before we are ready to receive them. If we commit ourselves to realizing God by a fixed date, then we are doomed to disappointment. If we are sincere, God is bound to give us realization at His choice Hour.

If you feel no enthusiasm or inspiration on a particular day, try to remember a joyful experience from your past. The joy you got from your previous achievements will carry you through. Very soon, you will not only reach, but transcend your previous height. You are not fooling yourself; you are only bringing happiness into your system, and this happiness is confidence. Try to feel that your problem is just a small obstacle that you will soon overcome.

One way to keep your enthusiasm is not to think of yourself as twenty-five or thirty or forty or fifty years old. Think of yourself as being only six or seven years old. A child does not sit; he just runs here and there. Identify yourself with the source of his enthusiasm.

Your outer smile can also help you to maintain enthusiasm. When you smile, you disarm your negative thoughts and feelings. While you are fighting and struggling with your enemy, if you smile, naturally your enemy will lose some of its strength. So play a trick on your enemy by smiling. This may sound absurd, but I assure you it is true. Just think of the negativity-world as an enemy whose strength can be weakened by your smile.

You should also have a sense of a clear goal. If you value the goal, then the goal itself will give you enthusiasm and freshness. If the goal is something worthwhile, then the goal itself will inwardly help you.

For meditation, like all other things, we need enthusiasm. If you are lacking enthusiasm, every day try sincerely, devotedly, and soulfully to feel that today is the last chance you will have to realize the Highest through your meditation. In the evening, when you see that you have not yet realized God, then console yourself. Think that tomorrow morning you will be given another chance. But when tomorrow morning dawns, again think, "Today is my last chance. Today, let me realize God, for I will not be given any other chance." Then you will try to do your best meditation. And even if you keep failing, you will not be depressed, because you will know that you have sincerely tried.

> *Your defeats in life's battlefield*
> *Will soon be ending,*
> *Because your mind is no longer indifferent*
> *To your heart's spontaneous enthusiasm.*

The Poison and the Antidote

Depression is a strong, undivine power that destroys the very breath of joy. Does depression help us in any way? Never. If you become depressed, then you are making your problems worse. You have to try to be as cheerful as possible. If you can be cheerful, then automatically half of your spiritual fever is gone.

Say to yourself: "If my source is God, the absolute, infinite Light, then someday I am bound to go back to my Source. During my stay on earth, I have unfortunately had some unhealthy and destructive experiences. Now I have to get rid of them. For that, I have to concentrate only on the divine things that will fulfill me, and not on the things that have stood in my way." In this way you can consciously bring down light into your entire system, and your dark depression-room will be transformed into an illumined room.

Let me give you an example. If you are disqualified from a race, what will you do? You will wait for another day and try again to reach the goal. If you stop trying just because you have had an unfortunate experience, you will never reach the goal. Likewise, a sad experience cannot be the ultimate experience. Take it as a passing cloud. You will definitely come out of this cloud. A wise person will take an unfortunate experience as a challenge, an opportunity to face an unpleasant reality with a cheerful smile. A fool will curse his fate and curse others. He will feel that this kind of misfortune happens only to him. Every experience in life can be meaningful and beneficial if we accept it properly.

If you know that you have taken depression-poison, you have to take the antidote: cheerfulness. You can do this by remembering that once upon a time you were cheerful, and what that cheerfulness did to help you.

Cheerful Gratitude

One special way to offer thanks or gratitude to God is through constant cheerfulness. We have to be happy in order to be truly grateful. In spiritual happiness, in the happiness that comes from self-giving and aspiration, gratitude looms large. When we have inner happiness, we do not have to search for gratitude here and there. In our devoted cheerfulness, in our soulful cheerfulness, we are bound to discover constantly increasing gratitude to the Supreme.

Cheerfulness is the conscious awareness of our inner divinity. When we are happy, we do not criticize God. On the contrary, we show our gratitude. You can maintain spontaneous delight by thinking of what you were and feeling gratitude for what you have already become. See the progress you have made and, on the strength of that progress, feel that you are running toward the goal.

Daring enthusiasm and abiding cheerfulness
Can accomplish everything on earth
Without fail.

CHAPTER TEN

The Descent of Compassion

Mine is the heart
That soulfully loves
Aspiration-sunrise.
Mine is the life
That unreservedly loves
Compassion-sunset.

Compassion is a spiritual magnet. It pulls us toward others. When we use our compassion and concern, we see that there is already an inner magnet operating.

Compassion is based on our sympathetic oneness. If

I have knee pain, I put my hand there and feel concern for my knee. Why? Because I feel that my knee is an integral part of my own existence. Similarly, if we feel oneness with someone, then compassion comes very easily. If we feel another's suffering as our own, if we are willing to be part of that person's life, then our compassion, concern, and other divine qualities immediately come to the fore.

Ordinarily, the so-called compassion offered by one individual to another involves a sense of separateness and inferiority. He who thinks he has compassion feels superior; he who receives this compassion feels inferior. Some people want to make us feel that they are purer and spiritually stronger than we are. They feel they are showing us compassion, but this is not compassion at all.

True compassion comes not from a feeling of superiority, but of oneness. If there is a feeling of oneness, everything that is divine, inspiring, illumining, and fulfilling is bound to be there. True compassion encompasses all our good qualities: our goodwill, our self-giving, our readiness and willingness to be of service to mankind. We will be able to offer these qualities if we have oneness with others.

Charity or Compassion?

The world believes that charity is an open door to Heaven, but it is mistaken. Charity does not necessarily indicate a sense of true concern and true love; when true concern and true love are wanting, the door of Heaven can never be open. It is not charity but the feeling of oneness that opens the door of Heaven. Without oneness, we are bound to the endless dance of superiority and inferiority.

Only oneness can give us satisfaction. When I give someone money or anything else, I should feel that I am giving in order to increase my own oneness with the world. I should feel that it is not I who am helping. On the contrary, I am being helped. This is not charity, but my self-giving in order to realize my higher self totally and integrally here in the world.

God's Compassionate Forgiveness

We can become more compassionate by thinking of Someone who is infinitely more compassionate than we are, and that is God. God's Compassion defies description. We make mistakes quite often, but He forgives and forgives. Similarly, if those around us make mistakes, we can easily offer them our compassion, since God is constantly showering His Compassion upon us. Once we realize that God is nothing but our own higher, more illumined Self, superiority and inferiority disappear into oneness, and we can claim God's infinite Compassion as our very own.

My morning begins
By claiming
God's Compassion-flooded Eye
As its own, very own.

Younger Brothers and Sisters

There is a great difference between compassion and pity. When we pity someone, we feel he is inferior to us. We stand millions of miles away or thousands of miles higher than the other person. But with compassion we just come to him and become one.

When you were seven or eight years old, you made many mistakes. You committed even Himalayan blunders. But your elders forgave you because you were a child. Automatically, compassion descends when you feel that somebody is a child and does not know better. If others are doing something wrong, feel that they are your little sisters and brothers. Today they do not know better, but someday they will start walking, then marching, then running toward their goal.

The Father's Protecting Arms

No matter where we are, God's Compassion-magnet is pulling us. To God's sorrow, we are afraid of being caught by this Compassion. Although many people love God, they are also afraid of Him. If they do something wrong, they feel God will punish them. God loves us unconditionally. When we practice spirituality, it should never be out of fear. Where there is oneness, there can be no fear.

If we fear God, how will we ever be able to reach Him or receive anything from Him? If a child is afraid of his father, he will avoid him. But if the child loves his father, then the child feels that the father will use his power not to strike him but to protect him.

If you consciously feel that you have done something wrong, then simply run to your eternal Father through your prayer and meditation. He will show you His utmost Compassion and nullify your mistake. God's Compassion will change your fate.

Let the Sun Shine

God's Grace is for everyone, like the rays of the sun. The sun is always there, but what do we do? We keep our doors and windows closed to shut out the sunlight. Then we do not get the blessing of the morning sun. Similarly, God's Grace is constantly descending, but we do not always keep our heart's door open to allow the Grace to enter into our system.

You can bring down the Compassion of the Supreme into your being just by crying like a child. When a child cries, he knows that his mother will come running to fulfill his need. If you cry soulfully from deep within, then your cry is bound to be heard by God the Mother and God the Father.

A single God-touch
From God's Compassion-Height
Can transform man's unimaginable
And countless weaknesses
Into God's own infinite,
Immortal, and omnipotent Power.

CHAPTER ELEVEN

Cultivating the Patience-Tree

> *Patience is the best*
> *Shock-absorber.*
> *Patience is the highest*
> *Peace-discoverer.*
> *Patience is the greatest*
> *Perfection-believer.*

Patience is not something passive. On the contrary, patience is dynamic; it always goes forward toward the goal. Patience has the steady movement of growth, and it is always accompanied by peace.

Patience is something that lengthens time. On earth,

our time is very limited. We should take patience as something that extends our time limit. While we are running a long distance, the goal seems far away and we want to reach it instantly. If we do not put a limit on the amount of time it should take us to reach our goal, then the light of patience can work in and through us.

If you feel that you are constantly fighting against time, then you are making a mistake. Feel instead that each moment is leading you toward your destination and that this progress in itself is a kind of partial goal. Rather than fighting against time, we should try our utmost to derive spiritual benefit from each second.

The road to our goal may be long. Sometimes you may feel that you are on an endless road through a barren desert, and that the goal is still impossibly far away. But do not give up walking just because the distance seems far. You have to be a divine soldier and march on bravely and untiringly. Patience is God's Power hidden in us to weather the teeming storms of life.

To develop patience, we have to feel that our goal wants us and needs us as much as we want and need it. The goal is ready to accept us and give us what it has, but it will do so in its own way at God's choice Hour.

If you can keep the goal of happiness in your mind, in your heart, in your breath, in all your actions, then you will develop patience. You have to tell yourself, "No matter how difficult the road is, if only I can arrive there, I will get so much joy." Your dream of happiness will give you patience and save you.

Weakness
or Strength?

Very often we forget the meaning of patience. We feel that it is a form of cowardice or a reluctant way of accepting the truth. We feel that because there is no other way left, we have to be patient. But tolerance and patience are not the same thing. Patience is a divine quality. Patience is the strengthening of our capacity. If we can be patient, then we can strengthen our inner willpower.

Patience is the soul-power
Concealed.
Patience is the heart-tower
Revealed.

Everything that we want to accomplish, we have to do on the strength of our sincerity. If we are students, we have to study. If we are seekers, we have to pray and meditate. Sincerity is of great importance.

To have a sincere longing does not mean that one cannot have patience. A high school student who sees that his brother has a master's degree may have a sincere longing for a master's degree as well. But he knows that time is a factor; it will take him years to get that degree. If he neglects his studies now, however, he will fail his examinations. Then how will he be able to go on to university?

It is important to progress gradually. If we lose our patience, we also lose our inspiration and we will never reach our goal. If we are always sincere and patient, we will find satisfaction even in our attempt. Our present satisfaction may not be the ultimate satisfaction, but we can rest assured that the ultimate satisfaction is bound to grow in us.

The Message of Perseverance

Once there was a young boy named Bopdeb, who was the worst possible student. His parents and teachers used to scold him mercilessly, but nothing did any good. Finally, his teachers gave up and threw him out of school. Bopdeb was such a fool that his parents did not want to keep him either. So poor Bopdeb, feeling miserable, left his home and went to the nearest village.

Bopdeb went to pray and meditate every day under a tree near a big pond. From there, he watched the village women carrying empty pitchers to the pond and filling them. Bopdeb noticed that the women would fill the pitchers, place them on the stone steps, and then go and bathe in the pond. After getting refreshed, they returned home with their pitchers of water.

One day when nobody was there, Bopdeb noticed that the part of the step on which the women put their pitchers was no longer level with the rest. Bopdeb said to himself, "Because the women have placed their pitchers here repeatedly, the stone is wearing down. If even a stone can wear down, then what is wrong with my brain?" From this experience, he came to understand patience and perseverance.

Bopdeb started praying and meditating more seriously, and a few days later he started reading his old Sanskrit grammar books again. He had been the worst possible student in Sanskrit, but now he was able to remember what he read. He continued his studies, and with patience and perseverance he eventually became the greatest Sanskrit scholar in India, especially in grammar.

Patience can never be imposed on us from outside. It is our own inner wealth. Like Bopdeb, you too will one day have the vision of what patience can achieve in your life. You will come to realize that your fondest dreams will be transformed into fruitful realities if you just know the secret of growing the patience-tree inside your heart.

> *In between your failure-tree*
> *And your triumph-tree,*
> *The tree that is growing*
> *Is known as your patience-tree.*

Never Give Up!

If you feel that your meditation is not as deep as it should be, never give up. We cannot eat the most delicious food every day, but still we eat. Similarly, when we meditate, we feed the soul, our inner being. Even if we cannot feed the soul most delightfully every day, we must not give up trying. It is better to feed the soul something than to allow it to starve. So never give up; always try to meditate.

We have to have the patience of a farmer. A farmer ploughs the field and cultivates the soil. Then he has to wait for God to give the rain, so that the seed can grow into a plant. Even so, in our life of aspiration, we have to practice meditation, but we also have to feel God's Grace descending on us like rain. When God's Grace descends and our human effort ascends, we will be able to meditate well all the time.

Patience and World-Transformation

When we go deep within, we see that the world is definitely evolving and progressing. In the outer world, we see fighting, battles, and wars. But we know that there is also another world, the inner world. When we aspire, we *do* see the evolution in our own nature and in others' lives. In short, we see the promise of perfection.

Perfection cannot come into existence overnight. It takes time. What we should do is cultivate soulful patience. To be patient does not mean that we are forced to surrender to the hard realities of life. No, patience is inner wisdom. Our inner wisdom tells us that it takes time to manifest divinity on the outer plane. What the entire world needs is soulful patience. Then the truth can grow in its own way.

Yesterday
Patience was the beginning
Of my perfection.
Today
Patience is the flowering
Of my satisfaction.

Cultivating the Patience-Tree

CHAPTER TWELVE

The Breath of a New Hope

Day and night I shall swim
In the sweetness-hope-river.

Often we see hope as something delicate and sweet—a soothing feeling which is a balm to our minds. But hope is something solid and strong. Inside hope there is a concealed power, for today's hope eventually turns into tomorrow's actuality.

If hope is just a mere wish, then your consciousness will not respond to it. But if it is something significant, like a vision that is trying to blossom inside your heart, your consciousness will be elevated. If it is real hope and not mere fantasy, then your consciousness-flower will blossom petal by petal with its nourishment.

Every day must come to you as a new hope, a new promise, a new aspiration. If you think that tomorrow will be just another day like all the days you have already seen, you will make no progress. Every day you have to energize yourself anew. For it is only with newness that you can succeed and transcend yourself.

The Eternal Beginner

Every seeker is a beginner. A beginner is one who has the inner urge to grow into something ever more divine, ever more illumining, and ever more fulfilling. The moment you want to make constant progress is the moment you become an eternal beginner. The dawn is the beginning of the new day; it symbolizes hope, illumination, and perfection. Every day the dawn plays the role of a beginner. It begins its journey at daybreak and ends its journey in the infinite sun. If you can feel that your whole being—your body, vital, mind, heart, and soul—represents the ever-blossoming dawn, then you will always remain an eternal beginner.

Every day we should feel that we have something new to accomplish. Every day we are advancing. You can transcend yourself only by discovering and maintaining your joy. If you discover your joy and maintain it, then you will always have the energy to go one more step.

May my mind every morning become
As beautiful as hope-dawn-rays.

Hope and Expectation

As hope is a power, so also is expectation. We expect many things from ourselves and from the world. Expecting good things has its justification. Unfortunately, expectation often tries to bargain with God. In the back of our minds, we expect that God will give us something just because we are praying and meditating. That kind of idea we must not cherish, for if our expectation is not fulfilled, we become frustrated, angry, and destructive.

Expectation is earthbound and limiting. We must

eventually play our role without any expectation of personal gratification whatsoever. At that time what will remain will be our sweetest hope. Hope is something sweet, divine, and encouraging. When we hope for something but we do not get it, we do not become angry or frustrated, because inside hope there is a divine touch. We know that our hope of today envisions the reality of tomorrow, and we can draw tremendous inner strength from this knowledge.

Peace begins
When expectation ends.

The Mother of Action

When we have human hope, the thing we are hoping for may or may not materialize. But when we have divine hope, there is an inner certainty that our hope will bear fruit, and we are inspired to work for the result. Divine hope is like a dream which comes at the end of the night bearing the promise that soon the day will dawn.

Let us say that today I have the hope that tomorrow

I will become a very sincere seeker. If it is just wishful thinking, when tomorrow dawns, it will find me fast asleep. But if it is divine hope, then immediately I will be inspired to act. I will feel that merely thinking or hoping that I will become something is not enough. I will enter into the field of activity. In this case, hope is the mother of action. If we enter into activity, then we will get the fulfillment of our hope or the transformation of our hope into reality.

Each sacred hope
Is a blessingful gift
From Heaven's heart.

A Burning Hope-Flame

If you want to live on earth, then you must have hope. If on a particular day there is no hope, then on that day you are dead. Believe in hope, grow into hope, and breathe in at every moment the fragrance and beauty of hope.

What can you do when you lose hope? You have to feel that your hope is bound to become a reality, precisely because you are in the world of aspiration. You are aspiring most sincerely, and most devotedly. You are doing the right thing. If the truth or the fulfillment that your hope has envisioned has not yet been able to manifest, do not worry. Only feel the necessity of burning the flame of your aspiration more brightly and more intensely.

Hope abides; therefore I abide.
Countless frustrations have not cowed me.
I am still alive, vibrant with life.
The black cloud will disappear,
The morning sun will appear once again
In all its supernal glory.

CHAPTER THIRTEEN

Peace: The Return to the Source

God has infinite children,
But the name of His fondest child
Is Peace.

At the dawn of his spiritual journey, almost every individual feels that peace is beyond reach. As the mounting flame of our aspiration climbs higher and higher, inner peace starts blossoming spontaneously in the very core of our being. One day we notice that we abide in the sea of peace, that we can never be separated from peace.

Peace is something tangible. It silences the outgoing

energy of the mind and feeds the aspiring heart. Peace is not merely the absence of quarreling and fighting. True peace is not affected by the roaring of the world, outer or inner. This sea of peace is at our command if we practice the spiritual life.

Peace of Mind

The first step toward peace of mind is to sincerely feel that we are not indispensable. We lack peace of mind because we feel that others need something from us, or we need something from others. We feel that if we do not do this or say that, then the world will collapse or everything will go wrong immediately. But the moment we can sincerely feel that we are not indispensable, we will not have to go anywhere to get peace, for peace will immediately come to us.

Another easy way to acquire peace of mind is to feel that nothing is unduly important. Everything and everyone on earth can fail us or desert us as long as we do not desert God and God does not desert us. God will never desert us because He is all Compassion, and even if we try our hardest, we will not be able to desert God because He is omnipresent. Except for God, nothing on earth is indispensable. If we can consciously and continuously make ourselves feel that He alone is indispensable, then nothing can take away our peace of mind.

Peace we achieve
When we do not expect anything
From the world,
But only give, give, and give
Unconditionally
What we have and what we are.

Our Peace Is Within

You cannot have peace in your outer life unless and until you have first established peace in your inner life. It is in the inner world that everything starts. Early in the morning, if you treasure a few divine thoughts before coming out of your home, then these thoughts will enter into your outer life as energizing, fulfilling realities.

Early in the morning, before you enter into the hustle and bustle of life, you should meditate regularly for fifteen minutes or half an hour. Then when you come out of your house into the world, you will be well protected—not with armor but with divine thoughts, divine ideas, and a divine goal.

When we meditate properly, we are bound to feel peace of mind. We are also bound to feel that we have a very large heart, which can house the entire world. We will feel spontaneous joy. Sometimes we may not know where this joy is coming from, but it actually comes from our own meditation.

Deep within us there is eternal silence, peace, and poise. When we are absolutely calm and quiet, we see that the inner life offers us its own energy. Our human mind may not understand this energy, because it does not originate in the mind. But our heart receives this energy from the soul.

During deep meditation, only the heart operates. The activity of the mind is totally silenced. The heart identifies with peace, and inside this peace we cultivate the inner truth and grow into the inner light.

I meditate
So that I can inundate
My entire being
With the omnipotent power of peace.

Peace Is Inner Wealth

In the morning, when you pray and meditate, feel that you have gained real wealth in the form of peace. As you keep your money inside your pocket, even so you can keep your peace inside your heart. With money-power you can buy whatever you want. Similarly, the spiritual power that you get from prayer and meditation is a real power. When people are quarreling, fighting, or behaving undivinely, just bring forward the inner peace and poise which you have kept inside your heart. Surcharge yourself once more with inner peace. The power of inner peace is infinitely more solid and concrete than any outer disturbance anybody can create on earth. Your inner peace can easily devour the irritation caused by others.

After you eat, you do not usually run or exercise. Similarly, when you receive something spiritual—peace, light, or bliss—you have to remain calm and quiet for some time. Before assimilation takes place, there is every possibility that the peace you have received will disappear. But once it is assimilated, it becomes part of your existence and you can never lose it. Mixing with people who are practicing spirituality and who meditate regularly will also help you to assimilate peace inside you.

Slowly and steadily you have to silence your mind
So that the peace-dove can nest in it.

Peace, Dynamism, and Strength

Peace itself is strength. If you have inner peace, you will have joy and delight when you enter into the outer world. The outer world can be under your control when you have peace of mind. Wherever you go, you will make your own peace.

In great power there is quietude. One who is outwardly strong, like a great boxer or a sovereign, has great peace and confidence inside him. If a person is not very strong, he clenches his fists and gets ready to defend himself. He has to show that he can fight. But when someone has boundless inner strength, he does not have to display it outwardly. He is relaxed because his inner strength has given him inner confidence. He is like a divine hero. At any moment, he can defeat the enemy or surmount any obstacle.

The Seven-Year-Old Heart

We say "peace of mind," but actually peace is never in the mind. When we want peace, we have to go beyond the realm of the mind. If you think that you are twenty years old or forty years old, then you will have to struggle with your mind to have even a glimpse of peace. But if you can feel that you are just seven years old, if you can have a childlike heart, then you will make the fastest progress.

There was a great Indian scientist named Dr. Satyendranath Bose. His name is truly immortal in the scientific world, not only in India but in other countries as well. He was not only great but also extremely good, kind, and humble. His heart was the heart of a child.

He had a special fondness for children and used to play many games with them. One game that he particularly liked was called Karam. One day he happened to be playing Karam with some children, and he was deeply absorbed in the game. A middle-aged man came by and for a long time was watching the game. After some time the scientist said to him, "What can I do for you?"

The man replied, "Tomorrow there will be a special meeting at our school. I would be so grateful if you would preside over the meeting."

Very politely the scientist responded, "No, I cannot. I am sorry. Please find somebody else."

Again the visitor urged, "Oh, we need you badly. There is nobody else as distinguished as you are. We shall be deeply honored if you come and preside over the meeting."

With utmost politeness the scientist replied: "I cannot come tomorrow at that hour because I am supposed to play with my friends here. Nothing gives me greater joy than to play with children. I have presided over hundreds and hundreds of meetings, and there I do not get any joy.

"I want joy, you want joy, everybody wants joy. To me, this game is infinitely more meaningful than the opportunity you are giving me to preside over a meeting, for I know that intellectual and argumentative people will come to that meeting, and they will bring their reasoning minds. I am fed up with the reasoning mind. I want only the heart, the sincere and pure heart, the oneness-heart. I find that kind of heart here, with my little friends.

"I have promised them that tomorrow I shall play with them, and I shall definitely do it. I want only to remain in the heart. I have played my role in the mind and now I am playing the role of my heart. Satisfaction is there, only there. Peace is there, only there."

O dreamers of peace, come.
Let us walk together.
O lovers of peace, come.
Let us run together.
O servers of peace, come.
Let us grow together.

Unless and until we have peace deep within us, we can never hope to have peace in the outer world. You and I create the world by the vibrations that we offer to it. If we can invoke peace and then offer it to somebody else, we will see how peace expands from one to two persons, and gradually to the world at large. Peace will come about in the world from the perfection of individuals. If you have peace, I have peace, he has peace, and she has peace, then automatically universal peace will dawn.

There are two wars: the inner war and the outer war. The inner war is the war that our soul fights against limitations, ignorance, doubt, and death. The outer war is the war that man fights against man, that nation fights against nation. These outer wars will come to an end only if the inner war stops first. We fight because deep inside us there is disharmony, fear, anxiety, and worry. When we have peace, joy, plenitude, and fulfillment, we shall not wage war.

*Right now fear, doubt, anxiety, tension, and disharmony
are reigning supreme.
But there shall come a time when this world of ours
will be flooded with peace.
Who is going to bring about this radical change?
It will be you: you and your sisters and brothers.
You and your oneness-heart will spread peace
throughout the length and breadth of the world.*

CHAPTER FOURTEEN

Our Lifelong Friends— Simplicity and Sincerity

Simplicity is my lifelong friend.
My simplicity-friend has cut down my desire-tree.
Sincerity is my lifelong friend.
My sincerity-friend has snapped my guilt-conscience-chain.

If we have a simple existence, we shall feel how happy and how fortunate we are. There are some people who are of the opinion that simplicity is almost tantamount to stupidity. But simplicity and stupidity are like the North Pole and the South Pole. One can be as simple as a child and, at the same time, one can have boundless knowledge, light, and wisdom.

In the course of our spiritual journey, just as we learn many things, so we must also unlearn many things. Each time we unlearn something, to that extent our life becomes simpler and we gain peace of mind. We unlearn fear, doubt, anxiety, jealousy, anger, and insecurity. We unlearn the teachings of the earthbound life, of the sophisticated mind with its disproportionate ego. The quicker we can unlearn these things, the wiser we shall become.

To have simplicity is to run toward God without darkness, worries, or impurity. God Himself is very simple. If we identify with His simplicity, confusion and complexity will disappear from our lives.

Simplicity shortens the road
That leads to God-discovery.

The Gardener

Our second Indian prime minister was very, very simple. From his appearance nobody could tell that he was a great leader. Only people who knew him well or those who were in the political world could recognize who he was. His outer appearance could fool anyone, since he was not tall and there was nothing about him physically that commanded respect and admiration from people. He always wore very simple clothes, and he was all simplicity and sincerity.

One day he was working in his garden, digging and planting all by himself. He was wearing very, very simple gardening clothes. A few middle-aged men came up to him and asked, "Can you tell us where the prime minister is?"

"Yes, I can," he replied. "Just wait. I will call him." Then he went into the house, washed his hands, put on a kurta and dhoti, and came out and stood in front of them.

"You!" they cried. "You have come again! You did not tell the prime minister that we are here? We want to see the prime minister, not you."

This time the gardener was more serious. He explained, "The prime minister is here. I am the prime minister."

"You are the prime minister of India?"

"Yes, I am!"

Some of them bowed down, some were shocked, and some felt miserable. "Oh, we thought you were just the gardener," they said.

Our Lifelong Friends—Simplicity and Sincerity

The prime minister replied: "I am so glad that you did not recognize me as the prime minister of India. I do not want the world to know me by my appearance but by my actions. I want to remain always simple, always humble."

The name of this prime minister was Lal Bahadur Shastri. He was simplicity and magnanimity incarnate. Lal Bahadur Shastri was without a single enemy. His own party admired him, and the opposition party equally admired him for his heart's nobility and his life's simplicity and purity.

Do you want to be happy?
Then make your life as soulfully simple
As sleeplessly breathing.

A Sincerity-Life

Sincerity goes hand in hand with simplicity. Sincerity is not something that has to be taught; it comes from deep within. We start with a cry, an inner cry. A child is not taught by its mother how to cry. It comes spontaneously.

When he needs milk, he cries. When we cry within most sincerely and soulfully, the Inner Pilot, the Supreme, listens to our cry. Then He illumines us in His own way.

We can always know whether we are sincere or not. When a feeling comes to the fore from the inmost recesses of our heart, it is bound to be sincere. This is not true in the case of the mind. The mind is constantly negating the ideas that have come directly from the mind itself. This moment we think that something is true and we are ready to fight for it, and the next moment we discover that it is absolutely false. When our own realization is dubious, if we build our assertion on it, then this assertion becomes totally insincere.

We have to offer the mind to the heart. If our focus of concentration is in our heart, then we will easily be able to feel that what is coming to the fore is all sincerity. Inside the heart is the soul. The soul cannot be anything else but a flood of sincerity. More than that, it is a flood of spirituality.

There is an easy way to remain in your heart. Feel that you have spread a net in which the entire world is caught. Inside this net you will give everyone joy and they will give you joy. When you think of playing a game, you become the heart. The heart is joy, the game is joy, and the player is joy. Finally, feel that there is somebody playing with you constantly and eternally. That person is God, the eternal Child.

Another way you can remain in the heart is to feel that inside you there is a divine child who is most luminous, infinitely more beautiful than any human being. This child is your soul. First think of your soul-child, and then think of its needs. It needs a place to live, and your heart is its most perfect abode.

Sincerity is the fertile ground in our heart.
Our sincerity is God's matchless Smile.
Our sincerity is God's peerless Pride.

Mahatma Gandhi's Matchless Sincerity

Once when Mahatma Gandhi was a young man, a friend of his needed money and asked if Gandhi could help him. At first Gandhi said, "I have no money." Then he conceded, "All right, I will see what I can do."

Gandhi stole a piece of gold from his brother and

sold it. Then he gave the money to his friend. Afterward, he felt miserable for having stolen something.

He always told his father everything. He kept no secrets from him. Although his father was very sick and bedridden, Gandhi wrote him a note, saying, "I stole a piece of gold from my brother and I feel sad and miserable. Please forgive me."

When his father read the note, he got up from his bed. Gandhi was afraid he was going to strike him. But there were tears in his father's eyes. Gandhi thought that his father was disappointed in him for having stolen something from his own brother, and that made him feel even more miserable. Finally, his father tore up the note and tears flooded his eyes.

Gandhi assured his father, "Father, I will never steal again. This is my first and last time. Please do not cry."

Deeply moved, his father replied, "I am crying, son, not because you stole something, but because of your sincerity. You are always so truthful. I have never known anyone as sincere as you. I am proud of you."

There are some people who are naturally sincere, and others who are naturally insincere. Those who, like Gandhi, are sincere from the dawn of their lives are blessed. But those who are insincere need not and must not curse themselves. They *can* be sincere if they want to. The moment they truly want to be sincere, God in His infinite Compassion will help them.

Strengthening Our Sincerity-Muscles

Each human being on earth has some sincerity, because inside each individual God abides. God has all divine qualities. Just because God is within us, sincerity is also within us. If we feel that we are lacking sincerity, we can develop this quality, just as an athlete develops his muscles.

One way to develop true sincerity is through soulful gratitude. If you can remember what you were before you began your spiritual journey, and see the difference between what you were then and what you are now, then automatically a spring of gratitude will well up inside you. Gratitude to whom? To the Supreme, for it is He who has inspired you and awakened your inner cry. Gratitude always embodies sincerity. A sincere heart and a gratitude-life must go together.

Again, you can become more sincere just by feeling

that sincerity gives you tremendous joy. The joy that we get from being sincere is unparalleled. Please try to remember the consequences in your life of insincerity. If you told a lie and were caught red-handed, then naturally you were embarrassed; you felt miserable. Even if you were not caught, still your conscience caught you. Now suppose you are about to say or do something wrong. Immediately stop and think, "How can I do this? It will take away all my joy." Then you will not do it. You will find that by abstaining from a wrong action, you will get infinitely more joy than if you had allowed yourself to do it. The spontaneous inner joy that comes from sincerity will always help you do the right thing.

Be sincere in your thoughts,
Be pure in your feelings.
You will not have to run after happiness.
Happiness will run after you.

CHAPTER FIFTEEN

Purity's Snow-white Blossoms

There is a flower deep inside your heart
And the name of that flower is purity.

Purity is the breath of God. If we have purity, then we can feel God as our very own. In purity our divinity can grow; in purity our true life can flourish and have its fulfillment here on earth.

If we can retain our purity, we will never lose anything worth keeping. Today we may have great thoughts or great inner power, but tomorrow we are bound to lose them if we are not pure.

There are many keys to open the door of purity,

but there is one key which is most effective, and that key is the absence of thought-waves in the mind. When the mind is calm and quiet, purity automatically dawns in the entire being. You can keep your mind pure by feeling constantly that you do not have a mind at all; you have only the flower-heart of a child. Feel every day for a few minutes that you have no mind. Say to yourself, "I have no mind. What I have is the heart." Then after some time, feel, "I do not have the heart. What I have is the soul."

When you say "I have no mind," this does not mean that you are becoming an animal. Far from it. You are only saying, "I do not care for this mind which is bringing me so much impurity and torturing me so much." When you say "I have the heart," you feel that the heart has purity. When you say "I have the soul," you are flooded with purity. Then after some time, you have to go deeper and further by saying not only "I have the soul," but also "I *am* the soul." The moment you say "I am the soul," and you meditate on this truth, your soul's infinite purity will enter into the heart. Then from the heart, purity will enter into the mind.

Another way to purify the mind is to think of the mind as a vessel that is full of dirty, filthy water. If we empty it, only then do we get the opportunity to gradually fill it up again with pure water. Always pray for purification of the mind. When we pray, purification takes place in our minds, and purity increases our God-receptivity. In fact, purity is nothing short of God-receptivity. Each time we pray, our inner vessel becomes large, larger, largest, and purity, beauty, light, and delight can enter into our vessel and sport together in the inmost recesses of our heart.

We can think of the mind as a dark room, a room that has not seen light for many, many years. We need someone who can bring light into this room. That person is the soul. We have to become the most intimate friend of our soul, who has the capacity to help us and the willingness to illumine anything that is dark within us. We have to consciously feel that we need the soul just as we need the body. If our need is sincere, then the soul will come forward and illumine our minds.

Is That So?

Today, or tomorrow, or in the distant future, you are bound to purify your life. But in the process of your self-transformation, if people do not understand or appreciate your pure life, please pay no attention to their criticism. At times we have seen that even a true spiritual Master, who is snow-white purity itself, has become a victim to the criticism of the ignorant world.

There was once a Zen Master who was very pure, and very illumined. Near the place where he lived there happened to be a food store. The owner of the store had a beautiful unmarried daughter. One day she was found to be with child. Her parents flew into a rage. They wanted to know who the father was, but she would not give them the name. After repeated scolding and harassment, she gave up and told them it was the Zen Master. The parents believed her and ran to the Zen Master, scolding him with a foul tongue. The Zen Master said, "Is that so?" This was his only comment.

When the child was born, they left the infant with him. He accepted the child and took care of it. By this time his reputation was totally ruined, and he was an object of mockery. Days ran into weeks, weeks into months, and months into years. But there is something called conscience in our human life, and the young girl was tortured by her conscience. One day she finally disclosed to her parents the name of the child's real father, a man who worked in the fish market. The parents again flew into a rage. At the same time, sorrow and humiliation tortured the household. They went running to the Zen Master, begged his pardon, narrated the whole story, and then took the child back. His only comment: "Is that so?"

The world may not understand or properly appreciate purity, but if Mother-Earth houses a single pure soul, her joy knows no bounds. She says, "Here, at last, is a soul I can rely upon."

The Fragrance of Purity-Flower

Inner purity depends to some extent on outer cleanliness. If you take a shower and wear clean clothes, if your body is clean and pure in every possible way, then it adds to your inner purity. Real inner purity is the constant remembrance of the Supreme, who is our Eternal Pilot. It is the feeling of having a living shrine deep in the inmost recesses of your heart. This is infinitely more difficult than taking a shower and keeping the body clean. But if you keep your outer life clean, then it definitely adds to your inner awareness and helps you considerably in re-membering the Eternal Pilot all the time.

If we invoke purity, then we are bound to bring our inner divinity to the fore. You have to feel that God is within you, purity is within you; only you have to reveal it. How do you reveal it? You reveal it by imagining within yourself the things that you see around you as pure.

You can purify your existence by feeling deep within yourself a beautiful rose or lotus, or any other flower that you like. A flower is all purity. Try to identify yourself with the consciousness of the flower or with the purity of the flower. Today it is imagination, but if you continue imagin-ing for five days, or ten days, or a month or two, then you are bound to see and feel the flower within you. First you may feel it, then you are bound to see the existence of the flower, and then automatically the fragrance and the purity of the flower will enter into you to purify you.

Look at a flower early in the morning and smell its fragrance. Then look straight at the morning sun, the early rising sun. How beautiful it is! In the evening, look at the moon. Do you see anything impure in it? Look at a candle flame and you will see that it is all purity; imagine that it is burning away all your impurities. Looking at anything which gives you the feeling of purity will help you purify your nature.

Another thing you can try is to consciously breathe in purity during your meditation. In the beginning you may have to use your imagination, but after a while you will see and feel that it is not imagination at all. When purity enters, it is like a current going from the sole of the feet to the crown of the head, and everything inside you is purified by it.

What you always have:
A fountain of flames.
What you always are:
A flower of purity.

Chanting

If you want to achieve overall purification of your nature, then chanting a mantra can be most effective. A mantra is an incantation; it can be a syllable, a word, a few words, or a sentence. Through chanting we can establish purity in our entire existence. The very utterance of the word "purity" can change both our inner and outer lives. Repeat the word "purity" 108 times daily, placing your right hand on your navel as you say it. You will see that abundant purity will enter into you and flow through you.

There is also another systematic way that chanting can be done. Select a mantra that appeals to you, such as "Aum"—which is the sacred sound of the Universe—or one of the Names of God. On the first day you can repeat your mantra five hundred times. The next day repeat it six hundred times. Increase the number by one hundred every day, until you reach twelve hundred, and then decrease the number by one hundred every day until you reach five hundred again. Continue this exercise, week by week, for a month. Whether you want to change your name or not, the world will give you a new name: purity.

While you are chanting, if you lose track of the number, no harm. Just continue with some likely number. The purpose of counting is to separate your consciousness from other things. While you are counting, you cannot think of anything else. At that time, try to enter into the world of silence which is deep inside the chanting. Then you will not have to count at all. Your consciousness will be focused on what you are repeating, and you will begin to feel that you are meditating only on the inner significance of the mantra.

It is through our constant inner cry that we achieve and increase purity. When our inner cry climbs up, we gradually illumine our whole being, and when illumination takes place, purity automatically enters into us. I have mentioned a few spiritual exercises that can help in acquiring purity. But the purity that lasts forever, the purity of the highest order, we get only from our inner cry for the highest Supreme.

Wherever you go, go with inspiration and aspiration.
Whatever you do, do with love and concern.
Whomever you see, see with purity's beauty
And responsibility's glory.

CHAPTER SIXTEEN

The Dance of Light

The dance of light
Awakens the wings of life
To soar into the Silence
Of the Absolute Supreme.

If we want to see anything in the outer world, in addition to keeping our eyes wide open, we need light—either sunlight or electric light or some other kind of light. But in the inner world, even with our eyes closed, we can see God, for God is the self-illumining Light.

Light is the life of the inner world. Light is the

power of the Supreme that transforms darkness. Anything that transforms our existence is light. Light is the life-breath of the Supreme.

The inner light actually comes from the soul; it is already inside us. The moment we can have free access to our soul, we will see that this light is coming to the fore to permeate our whole outer existence. We should always aim at illumination to transform our earthbound life into the Heaven-free world. Only one thing we need: a conscious awareness of the divine light which is ours. It is our birthright to realize and fulfill this inner light.

Ignorance and Illumination

Although light is the quality most needed to transform our lives, it is, unfortunately, the quality that is least wanted. We often cry for joy, peace, or power, but very rarely do we aspire for light. Why? Because we are afraid that light will expose our weaknesses and imperfections. But the inner light is not going to expose us. On the contrary, the inner light embraces humanity with all its imperfections and tries to illumine human ignorance so that the human life can be elevated into the divine life.

If we really care for illumination, we have to feel that we are growing from lesser light to more abundant light. If we always feel that we are deep in the sea of ignorance, then we will never, never come out of ignorance, for there is no end to the ignorance-sea. But if we feel that we are growing from an iota of light into the all-pervading, highest Light, the Light of the Supreme, then illumination immediately becomes easier and more spontaneous.

> *Feed your mind with your soul's*
> *Illumination-light-food.*
> *You will be the happiest person*
> *In God's entire creation.*

The Steadily Increasing Light

Full enlightenment is called God-realization. God-realization does not come all at once. It is a series of experiences. Sometimes when a seeker is in his highest meditation, he may get a kind of inner illumination. For half an hour or an hour his whole being may be illumined. But then, after an hour or two, he may become his same old self. Once again he may become a victim of desire and undivine qualities. On one level, illumination has taken place, but it is not the transcendental enlightenment of the Buddha or other God-realized Masters. When one gets God-realization, automatically infinite illumination takes place in one's outer as well as one's inner existence.

Sometimes when we speak of enlightenment, we mean that we have been in darkness about a particular subject for many years and now that particular place in our consciousness is enlightened. But this is just a spark of the boundless illumination of God-realization. It is only a temporary burst of light in the aspiring consciousness. After a short while it pales into insignificance, because there is no abiding reality in it. Abiding reality we get only with constant, eternal, and transcendental illumination, which is God-realization.

Our Light-Source

We should always bear in mind that we are of God and we are for God. Right now you may be a beginner; so for you God may not be a living reality. Sometimes you will only be able to imagine God, and most of the time, in spite of your best efforts, you will not feel the presence of God in yourself. Sometimes you may even forget the existence of God. But we all have a Source and that Source is infinite Light. If we can remember this, then we will feel a constant sense of satisfaction in our life.

We achieve the experience of light on the strength of our inner cry. When we work outwardly for material wealth or power, eventually we achieve success. If we want to do something or achieve something, we have to work for it. In the same way, if our goal is to achieve or become purest light, then our work is to cry like a child inwardly for inseparable oneness with the Supreme.

Spiritual light cannot be achieved by pulling or pushing. If we try to pull beyond our capacity of receptivity, our inner vessel will break. But if we develop great receptivity, then no matter how high our spiritual height or how much light we bring down from above, we will be able to assimilate it.

What are you waiting for?
The outer light is eagerly waiting
To show you the way.
The inner light is unconditionally waiting
To help you reach
The transcendental Goal.

The Inner Sun

Once the great Mughal Emperor Akbar asked his minister, "Birbal, for a long time I have been thinking of one question. I am sure you will be able to answer it. We see everything clearly in the sunlight, but is there anything that cannot be seen even with the help of sunlight?"

"Yes, Your Majesty," Birbal replied. "There is something that cannot be seen in the sunlight. Even the sunlight fails to illumine it."

"What is it, Birbal?"

"Your Majesty, it is the darkness of the human mind."

Birbal's answer is absolutely correct. The only question that Birbal might not have been in a position to answer is whether there is anything that can show us the ignorance of the mind and illumine it. We illumine the dark, unlit, obscure, impure mind by bringing to the fore our inner sun. Our inner sun, which is infinitely brighter than the physical sun, will dispel the ignorance-night of millennia.

Love the Truth. This is human illumination.
Become the Truth. This is divine illumination.
You are the Truth. This is the supreme illumination.

CHAPTER SEVENTEEN

The Wings of Joy

—

What is joy?
It is a bird that we all want
To catch.
It is the same bird that we all love
To see flying.

Happiness is love bubbling forth into the newness and fullness of true life. When we have a happy heart, we move forward. We dive deep within. We fly. Progress is in movement, and this movement comes only when we have joy and we become joy. When we are happy, we are making real progress.

As the Savior Christ taught, "The Kingdom of Heaven is within you." The Kingdom of Heaven is something that we can feel; it is a matter of our own inner achievement.

Heaven is a plane of consciousness that is full of peace and delight. We create Heaven with our divine thoughts. The moment we think something good, the moment we pray and meditate and try to offer the inner light that we have gained to the world at large, we begin to live in Heaven. Our aspiration, our mounting inner cry, leads us to this Kingdom. The higher we go beyond our limited consciousness, the quicker we shall enter into our deepest, infinite consciousness and the more intimately we shall see, feel, and possess the Kingdom of Heaven within ourselves. Yes, the Kingdom of Heaven is within us. Not only can we feel it, but, without the least possible doubt, we can become it.

The ever-mounting flame
Of my heart's aspiration-cry
Is the source of my life's
Ever-increasing joy and delight.

The Wings of Joy

Two thousand years ago, the Savior Christ gave us the supreme lesson: "Let Thy Will be done." Millions of prayers have been offered to God, but there can be no better, no greater, no more fulfilling prayer than this. If we love God, we become happy. If we serve God, we become happier. If we surrender our individual will to God's Will, we become happiest.

When something is God's Will, we will feel a kind of inner joy or satisfaction even before we start doing it. While working, we will also get joy. Finally, we will feel that we will be equally happy if our action is fruitful or fruitless. Ordinarily, we are happy only when success dawns and we see victory at the end of our journey. But if we can have the same kind of happiness, joy, and satisfaction whether we succeed or fail, and if we can cheerfully offer the result of our actions to God, then we will know that what we have done is God's Will.

Be Happy

Be happy!

You will grow into God's greatest blessing, His highest pride.

Be happy!

Yesterday's world wants you to enjoy its surrendering breath. Today's world wants you to enjoy its surrendered breath. Tomorrow's world wants you to enjoy its fulfilling breath.

Be happy!

Be happy in the morning with what you have.
Be happy in the evening with what you are.

Be happy!

Do not complain. Who complains? The blind beggar in you. When you complain, you dance in the mire of ignorance. When you do not complain, all conditions of the world are at your feet, and God gives you a new name: aspiration. Aspiration is the supreme wealth in the world of light and delight.

Be happy!

Do you want never to be poor? Then be happy.
Do you want ever to be great? Then be happy.

Be happy!

You will get what you like most.
You will be what you like best.

Be happy!

God sees in you His aspiring creation, His transforming realization, His illumining revelation, and His fulfilling manifestation.

Be happy!

God sees in you another God. God sees you as another God. God sees you and Him as one.

Real joy means immediate expansion. If we experience pure joy, immediately our heart expands. We feel that we are flying in the divine freedom-sky. The entire length and breadth of the world becomes ours, not for us to rule over, but as an expansion of our consciousness. We become reality and vastness.

If we are experiencing real joy, we can feel that God is pleased with us, for God's greatest achievement is our joy. When we are unhappy, miserable, and depressed, we house many undivine, negative forces. But when we are really happy, we give something truly valuable to God. God's deepest fulfillment is in receiving this gift from us.

What we call our joy, God calls our perfection. Each human being has come into the world with the message of perfection. Each human being on earth will one day realize the highest Truth. Each human being is destined to be fulfilled. It is the birthright of our soul.

About the Author

Born in Bengal, India, in 1931, and immersed from infancy in a deeply spiritual and loving family atmosphere, Sri Chinmoy spent his later youth, until the age of thirty-three, in a progressive spiritual community in the south of India. His childhood and youth experiences and training, coupled with a Western-style education, including a strong involvement in sports of all kinds (at which he excelled), have truly made him a spiritual teacher for the modern age.

Sri Chinmoy has studied as well as experienced the world's great religions, and he has embraced the wisdom and light of each one. The philosophy expressed in his writings comes from his personal inner explorations and his sublime encounters. He also draws from his spiritual identification (oneness) with the sad and happy experiences of truth-seekers and ordinary human beings alike.

Students of religious philosophy will see in Sri Chinmoy's writings the highest truths discovered by the seers, saints, and sages of every religious tradition throughout the ages. Students of humanity will be inspired, encouraged, and consoled by the timeless portrayals of Everyman and Everywoman in the stories, essays, and poems in this volume.